Presented To


From


Date

D1508743

## December 31

*The way of the Lord is a stronghold to the upright....*
*The righteous will never be shaken.*

PROVERBS 10:29-30 NASB

Webster defines hope, "to desire with expectation of fulfillment." To hope is to anticipate. It is more than dreaming, however. It is possessing within ourselves an expectation that someday there will be the fulfillment of that desire. It will become a reality. Hope always looks to the future, it's always on tiptoes. It keeps us going. It makes a dismal today bearable because it promises a brighter tomorrow.

—CHARLES R. SWINDOLL
*Dropping Your Guard*

Designed by UDG | Design Works, Sisters, Oregon.

# December 30

*He who receives Me receives Him who sent Me.*

MATTHEW 10:40

How do you simplify faith? How do you get rid of the clutter? How do you discover a joy worth waking up to? Simplify your faith by seeking God for yourself. No confusing ceremonies necessary. No mysterious rituals required. No elaborate channels of command or levels of access.

You have a Bible? You can study. You have a heart? You can pray. You have a mind. You can think.

—MAX LUCADO
*And the Angels were Silent*

## January 1

*He who promised is faithful.*

HEBREWS 10:23

A number of years ago, somebody counted the promises in the Bible and totaled up 7,474. I can't verify that number, but I do know that within the pages of the Bible there are thousands of promises that grab the reader and say, "Believe me! Accept me! Hold on to me!" And of all the promises in the Bible, the ones that often mean the most are the promises that offer hope at the end of affliction. Those promises that tell us, "It's worth it. Walk with Me. Trust Me. Wait with Me. I will reward you."

—CHARLES R. SWINDOLL
*Joseph*

# December 29

*I am with you always, even to the end of the age.*
MATTHEW 28:20

Remember, Christ is always near us. We should say nothing that we would not wish to say in His Presence. We should do nothing that we would not do in His Presence. We should go no place that we would not go in His Presence. But He is not with us just to judge or condemn us; He is near to comfort, protect, guide, encourage, strengthen, and help.

—BILLY GRAHAM
*The Secret of Happiness*

# *January 2*

*His merciful kindness is great toward us.*

PSALM 117:2

Kindness is invariably associated with mercy. It is impossible to be
kind without being merciful. Likewise to be merciful is to be kind. It
implies that there is a deep and genuine concern for another. This concern
is one of compassion and mercy. We are moved to be kind because we care.
Caring is the essence of God's selfless love expressed to another.

—PHILLIP KELLER
*A Gardener Looks at the Fruits of the Spirit*

# December 28

*He who believes in Me, as the Scripture has said, out
of his heart will flow rivers of living water.*

JOHN 7:38

Remember the words of Jesus to the Samaritan woman? "The water
I give will become a spring of water gushing up inside that person,
giving eternal life" (John 4:14 NCV). Jesus offers, not a singular drink
of water, but a perpetual artesian well! And the well isn't a hole in your
backyard but the Holy Spirit of God in your heart.

—MAX LUCADO
*He Chose the Nails*

# January 3

*In Your hand is power and might; in Your hand it is
to make great and to give strength to all.*

I CHRONICLES 29:12

The crowning jewel of Creation was man himself. He was created for a distinct purpose. If the purpose is lived out, life is fulfilling. If the purpose is rejected or ignored, life will never be what it was meant to be. Apart from the Creator's purpose, you and I are like a light bulb lying in a meaningless, useless state. We need to fit into the Creator's original design, plugging into the power source—our relationship with Him—if our lives are to be what they were meant to be.

—ANNE GRAHAM LOTZ
*God's Story*

# December 27

*The street of the city was pure gold, like transparent glass.*

REVELATION 21:21

The Bible tells us that when we get to Heaven all of our sins and flaws will fall away, and we will be like Jesus. With our unique personalities and characteristics, every single one of us is going to perfectly reflect the character of Christ. And as we walk on streets that reflect like mirrors, every step we take and every move we make is going to bring glory to Him.

—ANNE GRAHAM LOTZ
*Heaven: My Father's House*

# *January 4*

*You cannot add any time to your life by worrying about it.*
MATTHEW 6:27 NCV

A nxiety is an expensive habit. Of course, it might be worth the cost if it worked. But it doesn't. Our frets are futile.

Worry has never brightened a day, solved a problem, or cured a disease.

God leads us. God will do the right thing at the right time. And what a difference that makes.

— *MAX LUCADO*
*Traveling Light*

# December 26

*Peace I leave with you, My peace I give to you;*
*not as the world gives do I give to you.*

JOHN 14:27

Jesus didn't leave a material inheritance to His disciples. All He had when He died was a robe, which went to the Roman soldiers; His mother, whom He turned over to His brother John; His body, which He gave to Joseph of Arimathea; and His Spirit, which returned to His Father.

But Jesus willed His followers something more valuable than gold, more enduring than vast landholdings and more to be desired than palaces of marble—He willed us His peace.

—BILLY GRAHAM
*The Secret of Happiness*

# January 5

*If the Son makes you free, you shall be free indeed.*
JOHN 8:36

This freeing of the self is the real purpose of righteousness: the rightness that God asks of His children. Yet all too often we have thought that righteousness means the end of all our fun and freedom. Nothing could be further from the truth. God's love means sheer goodwill for us. Each of us can find the truth for ourselves only as we, step by step, walk the Faith Road, for God sees to it that sight never precedes faith.

— CATHERINE MARSHALL
*Moments that Matter*

# December 25

*They shall obtain joy and gladness and sorrow and sighing shall flee away.*

ISAIAH 35:10

The black, velvety sky was clear and studded with sparkling stars that had looked down on Earth since the beginning of time. On the clear night air, sound traveled easily and somewhere from the direction of the village inn someone slammed a door.

The Seed of the woman, who would open heaven's gate and welcome any and all who place their faith in Him…had been given!

The Hope that was born that night continues to radiate down through the years until it envelops your heart and mine.

—ANNE GRAHAM LOTZ
*God's Story*

# January 6

*If any of you lacks wisdom, let him ask of God, who gives to all liberally and without reproach, and it will be given to him.*

JAMES 1:5

If you are smack-dab in the middle of a crisis today, cry out to God. Tell Him exactly how you feel. He can handle it. Someone once told me that God is not embarrassed by the honesty of our prayers. Get gut-level honest with God and tell Him how badly you hurt, how angry you are, and that you need His help to get through this crisis. Don't worry about God—He can deal with this.

—JOHN HULL AND TIM ELMORE
*Pivotal Praying*

# December 24

*I will meditate on the glorious splendor of Your majesty, and on Your wondrous works.*

PSALM 145:5

Has it been a while since you stared at the heavens in speechless amazement? Has it been awhile since you realized God's divinity and your carnality? If it has, then you need to know something. He is still there. He hasn't left. Under all those papers and books and reports and years. In the midst of all those voices and faces and memories and pictures, He is still there.

Do yourself a favor. Stand before Him again.

—MAX LUCADO
*Six Hours, One Day*

## January 7

*The eyes of the Lord are on the righteous,*
*and His ears are open to their prayers.*

I PETER 3:12

God knows what it is to need. The One who caused water to burst from the rocks for the Israelites had to ask a woman to bring Him a simple drink from a well. The One robed in splendor in the courts of heaven was stripped naked and nailed to a cross. The One who created the galaxies had to build fires to shield Himself from the winter cold. Meeting human need, then, is very much on God's agenda. Human needs are not irrelevant or unspiritual.

—MICHAEL YOUSSEF
*The Prayer that God Answers*

# December 23

*Therefore by their fruits you will know them.*

MATTHEW 7:20

Fruit production in our Christian experience, just as in an orchard or garden, is not something that goes on with great fanfare, noise or theatrics. From the opening of the first tiny bud under the impulse of spring sunshine, to the perfect ripening of the fully formed fruit beneath late Indian summer skies, the whole process goes on quietly, serenely, and surely. It is the Spirit of God who by His presence within guarantees growth, maturity, and conformity to Christ.

—PHILLIP KELLER

*A Gardener Looks at the Fruits of the Spirit*

# January 8

*As He who called you is holy, you also be holy in all your conduct.*

I PETER 1:15

No human is holy in himself. Holiness is foreign to us. It is alien. That is why we require the righteousness of Another to cover our moral nakedness. The Holy One has given us the holiness we need in the cloak of Christ's righteousness.

—R. C. SPROUL
*In the Presence of God*

## December 22

*Happy are the people whose God is the Lord!*

PSALM 144:15

We are God's treasure! When God the Father looked throughout the universe for something to give His only Son in reward for what He had accomplished on earth, the Father handpicked you! You are the Father's priceless gift of love to the Son!

—ANNE GRAHAM LOTZ
*Heaven: My Father's House*

# January 9

*We can enter through a new and living way that Jesus opened for us. It leads through the curtain—Christ's body.*

HEBREWS 10:20 NCV

To the original readers, those last four words were explosive: "the curtain—Christ's body." According to the writer, the curtain equals Jesus. Hence, whatever happened to the flesh of Jesus happened to the curtain. What happened to His flesh? It was torn. Torn by the whips, torn by the thorns. Torn by the weight of the cross and the point of the nails. But in the horror of His torn flesh, we find the splendor of the open door.... We are welcome to enter into God's presence—any day, any time.

—MAX LUCADO
*He Chose the Nails*

# December 21

*As a father pities his children, so the Lord pities those who fear Him.*

PSALM 103:13

Are you feeling crushed and confused, misunderstood and beaten down? Resist the temptation to roll up your sleeves and muster a self-imposed recovery plan. This is your opportunity! Rather than fighting back, surrender. Embrace your weakness. Tell your heavenly Father you are trusting in the strength of His power. *Look up!*

—CHARLES R. SWINDOLL
*Paul: A Man of Grace and Grit*

# January 10

*Lord, who may abide in Your tabernacle? He who walks uprightly,
and works righteousness, and speaks the truth in his heart.*

PSALM 15:1-2

You're invited to live with the Lord, to make yourself at home
with Him. But there's a particular way to get there.

Walk uprightly. Work righteousness. Speak the truth in your heart.

In short, let your life be cleansed and free and full of all good things. Be
saturated in His Spirit.

—PETER WALLACE
*What the Psalmist Is Saying to You*

*For the grace of God that brings salvation has appeared to all men.*
TITUS 2:11

A s moments go, that one appeared no different than any others.... It came and went.... It was one of the countless moments that have marked time since eternity became measurable.

But in reality, that particular moment was like none other. For through that segment of time a spectacular thing occurred. God became a man. While the creatures of earth walked unaware, Divinity arrived.

— MAX LUCADO
*God Came Near*

# January 11

*I have loved you with an everlasting love; therefore with lovingkindness I have drawn you.*

JEREMIAH 31:3

We get in a hurry when we don't wait on the Lord. We jump ahead and do rash things. We shoot from the hip. We run off at the mouth, saying things that we later regret. But when we have sufficiently waited on the Lord, He gets full control of our spirit. At such moments, we're like a glove, and His hand is moving us wherever He pleases.

—*CHARLES R. SWINDOLL*

*Esther*

# December 19

*The Son of Man will come in the glory of His Father with His angels, and then He will reward each according to his works.*

MATTHEW 16:27

If with courage and joy we pour ourselves out for God and for others for His sake, it is not possible to lose, in any final sense, anything worth keeping. We will lose ourselves and our selfishness. We will gain everything worth having.

—ELISABETH ELLIOT
*The Path of Loneliness*

# January 12

*So you shall serve the Lord your God,*
*and He will bless your bread and your water.*

EXODUS 23:25

You may find temporary satisfaction in things and people, but permanent, deep, full satisfaction of your very being is only found in a right relationship with God for Whom you were created.

Not only is your *being* created for God, but your *doing* is created for God also. You and I were created for commitment to serve God.

—ANNE GRAHAM LOTZ
*God's Story*

# December 18

*Those who sow in tears shall reap in joy.*

PSALM 126:5

God does not waste our tears. He counts and invests each one. Tears of brokenness water the dry and parched places in our souls and in our world.

One more ingredient is essential though if our tears are to produce fruit: *sowing.*

In the midst of pain, we are to give. In the midst of heartache, we are to serve.

Brokenness - service = bitterness

Brokenness + service = fruitfulness

—ALICIA BRITT CHOLE
*Pure Joy*

# *January 13*

*God is my strength and power, and He makes my way perfect.*

II SAMUEL 22:33

For the man or woman who recognizes the claim of Christ and gives allegiance to His absolute ownership, there comes the question of bearing His mark. The mark of the cross is what should identify us. The question is—does it?

Basically what it amounts to is this: A person exchanges the fickle fortunes of living life by sheer whimsy for the more productive and satisfying adventure of being guided by God.

—PHILLIP KELLER
*A Shepherd Looks at Psalm 23*

# December 17

*Present your bodies a living sacrifice, holy, acceptable
to God, which is your reasonable service.*

ROMANS 12:1

L ife is full of journeys. Some are dull excursions we grudgingly take out of sheer duty. Others are thrilling adventures we embark on with eyes of faith. But changes await you…changes in you. No journey is more life changing than your inner spiritual journey back to the Cross. In all your travels, have you gone there? If not, are you willing to take that first step? It's a journey you will never regret. I can assure you, and one you will never forget.

—CHARLES R. SWINDOLL
*Paul: A Man of Grace and Grit*

## January 14

*A faithful man will abound with blessings.*

PROVERBS 28:20

Waiting is our destiny as creatures who cannot by themselves bring about what they hope for. We wait in the darkness for a flame we cannot light, we wait in fear for a happy ending we cannot write. We wait for a "not yet" that feels like a "not even." Waiting is the hardest work of hope.

—LEWIS SMEDES
*Keeping Hope Alive*

## December 16

*If anyone serves Me, let him follow Me.*

JOHN 12:26

God deals differently with each of us. He knows no "typical" case. He seeks us out at a point in our own need and longing and runs down the road to meet us. This individualized treatment should delight rather than confuse us, because it so clearly reveals the highly personal quality of God's love and concern.

—CATHERINE MARSHALL
*Moments that Matter*

# January 15

*To Him who is able to establish you…to God, alone wise, be glory through Jesus Christ forever.*

ROMANS 16:25-27

God alone is the Source of all wisdom. A person may have natural logic. He or she may have natural wisdom. But logic and wisdom err in that they will always put the individual person first. They are not supernatural wisdom. Supernatural wisdom comes only from God, and it comes through Jesus Christ the personification of God's wisdom to us.

—*LARRY LEA*
*Wisdom: The Gift Worth Seeking*

# *December 15*

*The sufferings of this present time are not worthy to be
compared with the glory which shall be revealed in us.*

ROMANS 8 :18

A s humans we tend to focus on the immediate. Yet all the while, God is
orchestrating the entirety of our lives, using specific details, specific
people, specific circumstances, specific words. We tend to look at one piece
of the puzzle, while God sees the whole picture as well as the detailed
specifics within each piece. We see things in black and white, while God
sees things in panoramic color.

—JOHN HULL AND TIM ELMORE
*Pivotal Praying*

# January 16

*But You, O Lord, are a God full of compassion, and gracious,
longsuffering and abundant in mercy and truth.*

PSALM 86:15

Like the father in the parable about the Prodigal Son, God is waiting, looking, His eyes glued to the horizon searching for us. When He sees us, though He is a dignified patriarch, He lifts up His garment and shamelessly gallops toward us, as we come trudging toward Him with our load of guilt and despair. He wraps us in His arms and smothers us with kisses.

This is not new behavior for God. He has looked at people with compassion for centuries.

—PAUL E. MILLER
*Love Walked Among Us*

# December 14

*Those who are wise shall shine like the brightness of the firmament.*

DANIEL 12:3

I am amazed to see, how frequently the giving of gifts is mentioned in the Bible…. Rebekah accepts gifts of jewelry and clothing, symbolic of her acceptance of Isaac as her husband. Jacob tries to give a lavish present of livestock to the brother he has wronged…. Wise Men bring gifts to an Infant—gold, which acknowledges their King, frankincense their God, myrrh their Redeemer.

—CATHERINE MARSHALL
*Moments that Matter*

# January 17

*It is to your advantage that I go away; for if I do not go away, the Helper will not come to you; but if I depart, I will send Him to you.*

JOHN 16:7

When Jesus left this world He went to the Father. His ascension was to a certain place for a particular reason. To ascend did not mean merely "to go up." He was being elevated to the right hand of the Father. The seat He occupies on His departure is the royal throne of cosmic authority. It is the office of the King of the Kings and the Lord of the Lords.

— R. C. SPROUL
*In the Presence of God*

## December 13

*He was wounded for our transgressions, He was bruised for our iniquities.*
ISAIAH 53:5

There is no way our little minds can comprehend the love of God. But that didn't keep Him from coming....

From the cradle in Bethlehem to the cross in Jerusalem we've pondered the love of our Father. What can you say to that kind of emotion? Upon learning that God would rather die than live without you, how do you react? How can you begin to explain such passion?

—MAX LUCADO
*In the Grip of Grace*

# January 18

*I will turn their mourning to joy, will comfort them,*
*and make them rejoice rather than sorrow.*

JEREMIAH 31:13

Human beings by nature want to hug life and hold onto it, choke it down, save it and keep it. But Jesus taught there's only one way to know life's meaning: We gain happiness by letting go of this life.

What is joy? It is Christ.

— *CALVIN MILLER*
*Into the Depths of God*

# December 12

*God is a safe place to hide, ready to help when we need Him.*

PSALM 46:1, THE MESSAGE

Have you ever asked God for something that He did not give you? At first, you might have felt slighted or upset, but perhaps much later you saw the reason why God said no. God promises to give only what is good for you and no less. Why? The Lord loves you with an affection beyond imagination, and He fashioned every intricate fiber of your being. It makes sense, then, that He knows exactly what you need and what blessings would benefit you.

— CHARLES STANLEY
*Into His Presence*

## January 19

*If you keep My commandments,*
*you will abide in My love.*

JOHN 15:10

Learning to pray is learning to trust the wisdom, the power, and the love of our Heavenly Father, always so far beyond our dreams. He knows our need and knows ways to meet it that have never entered our heads. Things we feel sure we need for happiness may often lead to our ruin. Things we think will ruin us,…if we believe what the Father tells us and surrender ourselves into His strong arms, bring us deliverance and joy.

—ELISABETH ELLIOT
*Keep a Quiet Head*

## December 11

*No eye has seen, no ear has heard, no mind has conceived
what God has prepared for those who love Him.*

I CORINTHIANS 2:9 NIV

Paul simply means we cannot outdream God. What is at the end of our personal journeys? Something beyond our wildest imagination.

—BRENT CURTIS AND JOHN ELDREDGE
*The Sacred Romance*

# January 20

*It is no longer I who live, but it is Christ who lives in me.*

GALATIANS 2:19

L ittle by little we are changed by this daily crucifixion of the will. Changed, not like a tornado changes things, but like a grain of sand in an oyster changes things. New graces emerge: new ability to cast all our care upon God, new joy at the success of others, new hope in a God who is good…. God is not destroying the will but transforming it so that over a process of time and experience we can freely will what God wills.

—*RICHARD FOSTER*
*Prayer: Finding the Head's True Home*

# December 10

*God so loved the world that He gave His only begotten Son, that whoever believes in Him should not perish hut have everlasting life.*

JOHN 3:16

An ordinary night with ordinary sheep and ordinary shepherds. And were it not for a God who loves to hook an "extra" on the front of the ordinary, the night would have gone unnoticed. The sheep would have been forgotten, and the shepherds would have slept the night away.

But God dances amidst the common. And that night He did a waltz....

The night was ordinary no more.

—MAX LUCADO
*The Applause of Heaven*

# January 21

*You have filled my heart with greater joy than when their grain and new wine abound.*

PSALM 4:7 NIV

In David's time, the hope of many rested upon the outcome of the year's harvest. If the crops were plentiful, the community rejoiced. If the crops failed, the community despaired.

But David experienced a joy that flourished even when crops perished. He treasured a joy that thrived even through drought. David knew a joy that was pure. Such joy flows from one source: the living God.

—ALICIA BRITT CHOLE
*Pure Joy*

# December 9

*One thing I have desired of the Lord,…that I may dwell in the house of
the Lord all the days of my life, to behold the beauty of the Lord.*

PSALM 27:4

The beauty of God describes His moral character. God is holy, pure,
just, loving, wise, longsuffering, merciful, gracious, and so much
more; and these attributes exist in perfect harmony and are manifested
in perfectly balanced ways. God's beauty is the beauty of perfection, a
beauty that borrows from nothing and no one and to which nothing or no
one may be compared.

—WARREN W. WIERSEBE
*The Twenty Essential Qualities*

# January 22

*Let them shout for joy and be glad, who favor my righteous cause.*

PSALM 35:27

God is a deeply, profoundly passionate person. Zeal consumes Him. It is the secret of His life, the writer of Hebrews says. The "joy set before him" enabled Jesus to endure the agony of the Cross (Heb. 12:2, NIV). In other words, His profound desire for something greater sustained Him at the moment of His deepest mal.

—JOHN ELDREDGE
*The Journey of Desire*

# December 8

*Come to me, all you who labor and are heavy laden, and I will give you rest.*

MATTHEW 11 :28

Most of us think of spiritual progress as requiring us to do more, even as our heart cries out to us to lay our burdens down. We *renew* our efforts at Bible study, Scripture memory, and Christian service, fearing that we will be discovered in our weakness and need. We try to use whatever small story we have been living incompetence, gifted speaking, service to others, and so on—to cross the chasm between living in the flesh and living spiritually, when only Christ can carry us to rest.

—BRENT CURTIS AND JOHN ELDREDGE
*The Sacred Romance*

# January 23

*Do not grieve the Holy Spirit of God, by whom you
were sealed for the day of redemption.*

EPHESIANS 4:30

If you are like I am, you love surprises. The greatest surprise you will ever experience is the surprising joy that comes when God, through His Holy Spirit, fills your heart to the fullest. Your days will be filled with more than you would ever ask or even dream of.

—NEIL CLARK WARREN
*God Said It, Don't Sweat It*

# December 7

*He lays the beams of His upper chambers in the waters, Who makes the clouds His chariot, Who walks on the wings of the wind, Who makes His angels spirits.*

PSALM 104:3-4

God establishes the rain that waters and nourishes the earth in the clouds of the sky. He moves around and above us on a chariot of clouds, "on the wings of the wind."

He summons and sends out His angelic ministers to work His will in the earth—protecting, guiding, providing.

He is working continually, establishing His will, answering prayers, touching lives, healing sick hearts. Even in your life.

—PETER WALLACE
*What the Psalmist Is Saying to You*

# January 24

*Let all those rejoice who put their trust in You; let them*
*ever shout for joy, because You defend them.*

PSALM 5:11

God told us from the very beginning that in love—His love—we find the answer to all our needs as well as healing for our broken souls.

When your heart is anchored to the heart of Jesus Christ, you will find Him near and always eager to confirm His personal love for you. The love of the world will pass away, but God's love is guaranteed never to fade. He is the Source of all true, lasting love.

*—CHARLES STANLEY*
*Into His Presence*

# December 6

*This hope we have as an anchor of the soul, a hope both sure and steadfast.*

HEBREWS 6:19 NASB

God keeps His promises. It's a major part of His immutable nature. He doesn't hold out hope with nice-sounding words, then renege on what He said He would do. God is neither fickle nor moody. And He never lies. As my own father used to say of people with integrity. "His word is His bond."

—CHARLES R. SWINDOLL

*Elijah*

# January 25

*You have been born again, not of perishable seed, but of imperishable, through the living and enduring word of God.*

1 PETER 1:23 NIV

The only way to get into the human family is to be born. Everybody you meet has a birthday every year because birth is the method God has ordained for transmitting human life from one generation to the next.

What's true of the physical is also true of the spiritual: the only way to possess God's life and enter God's family is through birth.

—WARREN W. WIERSEBE

*The Twenty Essential Qualities*

## December 5

*Where your treasure is, there your heart will be also.*

MATTHEW 6:21

The physical body you live in. The family you were born into. The opportunities that have crossed your path. The faith you have. All are ultimately from God. Even the breath you breathe every minute is a gift from God…. God has given you these gifts to see what you will do with them. He is watching to see if you are greedy. He is watching to see if you are going to trust money more than you trust Him.

— *LARRY LEA*
*Wisdom: The Gift Worth Seeking*

## January 26

*Pray without ceasing....He who calls you is faithful, who also will do it.*

I THESSALONIANS 5:17,24

Jesus taught that answered prayer requires persistence. There may be a period when the door of blessing on which we hammer in prayer remains shut to us. Yet if we persist in knocking, the promise is that God will eventually open the door.

—CATHERINE MARSHALL
*Moments that Matter*

# December 4

*But the Lord is the true God; He is the living God and the everlasting King.*

JEREMIAH 10:10

Looking down over the battlements of heaven God saw this planet swinging in space—doomed, damned, crushed, and bound for hell. He saw you and me struggling beneath our load of sin. He made His decision. The angelic hosts bowed in humility and awe as heaven's Lord of Lords, who could speak worlds into space, got into His jeweled chariot, went back through pearly gates, across the steep of the skies, and on a black Judean night, while the stars sang together and the escorting angels chanted His praise, stepped out of the chariot, threw off His robes, and became man!

—BILLY GRAHAM
*Peace with God*

# January 27

*Your testimonies are wonderful; therefore my soul keeps them.*

PSALM 119:129

There are those who regard the Bible principally as the history of Israel. Others admit that it sets forth the soundest ethics ever enunciated. But these things, important as they are, are only incidental to the real theme of the Bible, which is the story of God's redemption as it exists in Jesus Christ.

Those who read the Scriptures as magnificent literature, breath-taking poetry or history, and overlook the story of Salvation, miss the Bible's real meaning and message.

— BILLY GRAHAM
*Peace with God*

# December 3

*The mercy of the Lord is from everlasting to everlasting on those who fear Him.*

PSALM 103:17

Those who saw Jesus—really saw Him—knew there was something different. At His touch blind beggars saw. At His command crippled legs walked. At His embrace empty lives filled with vision. He fed thousands with one basket. He stilled a storm with one command. He raised the dead with one proclamation. He changed lives with one request. He rerouted the history of the world with one life, lived in one country, was born in one manger, and died on one hill.

—MAX LUCADO
*And the Angels were Silent*

# January 28

*[They] nailed Him to a cross…This was God's plan which He had made long ago.*
ACTS 2:23 NCV

Jesus' death was not the result of a panicking cosmological engineer. The cross wasn't a tragic surprise. Calvary was not a knee-jerk response to a world plummeting toward destruction. It wasn't a patch-up job or a stop-gap measure…. The moment the forbidden fruit touched the lips of Eve, the shadow of a cross appeared on the horizon. And between that moment and the moment the man with the mallet placed the spike against the wrist of God, a master plan was fulfilled.

—*MAX LUCADO*
*God Came Near*

## December 2

*He who overcomes shall inherit all things, and I will
be his God and he shall be My son.*

REVELATION 21:7

What shall it be like in heaven?

Some of our truest images of ourselves in heaven, it seems to me, are
stirred up by bread-and-butter pleasures we enjoy here. Have a thigh-
thumping laugh at a ridiculous story, and you get a sharp snap of yourself
happy in heaven. Let a piece of soul music send shivers down your spine,
and you have an image of your capacity for beauty in heaven…. Maybe the
happiest memories of ourselves on earth are our clearest images of what
we shall be in heaven.

—LEWIS SMEDES
*Keeping Hope Alive*

# January 29

*Since He Himself was tempted,…He is able to come
to the aid of those who are tempted.*

HEBREWS 2:18 NASB

Having been swamped by sin all our lives, struggling to find our way to the top of the water to breathe, we can find great hope in the ability God gives us not only to breathe but to swim freely. You see, Christ not only lived an exemplary life, He also makes it possible for us to do the same. He gives us His pattern to follow *without* while at the same time providing the needed power *within*.

—*CHARLES R. SWINDOLL*

*Joseph*

# December 1

*If they could be made God's people by what they did, then
God's gift of grace would not really be a gift.*

ROMANS 11:6 NCV

To whom does God *offer* His gift? To the brightest? The most beautiful
or the most charming? No. His gift is for us all—beggars and bankers,
clergy and clerks, judges and janitors. All God's children.

And He wants us so badly, He'll take us in any condition—"as is" reads
the tag on our collars…. He wants us *now*.

—MAX LUCADO

*No Wonder They Call Him the Savior*

# January 30

*I stand at the door and knock.*
*If anyone hears My voice and opens the door, I will come in to him.*

REVELATION 3:20

God's invitation is clear and nonnegotiable…Isn't it incredible that God leaves the choice to us?

Think about it. There are many things in life we can't choose. We can't, for example, choose the weather. We can't control the economy. We can't choose whether or not we are born with a big nose or blue eyes or a lot of hair…. But we can choose where we spend eternity. The big choice, God leaves to us.

—MAX LUCADO
*And the Angels Were Silent*

# November 30

*You wove me in my mother's womb. I will give thanks to You, for I am fearfully and wonderfully made.*

PSALM 139:13-14 NASB

God reached into my life when I was merely a tiny embryo and began to shape me within. He originated me. He began to put me together while I was still in the soft silence of my mother's womb…. Mother Nature didn't make me. Fate did *not* shape me, neither was I just a biological combination of mother and dad in a *moment* of sexual passion. Nor was I conceived through blind chance. You, God (and *no* other), made me!

—*CHARLES R. SWINDOLL*
*Day by Day*

# January 31

*In all their distress, He too was distressed;...He lifted them up and carried them.*

ISAIAH 63:9 NIV

The solution to loneliness is not to give in or give up or do what everyone else does or go where everyone else goes or look like and speak like and think like and act like the world around you so you won't stand out so sharply from the crowd. The solution is not to withdraw into an uninvolved, inactive life. The solution is found when we discover meaning in the midst of loneliness as God Himself shares our loneliness while we walk with and work for Him.

—ANNE GRAHAM LOTZ
*God's Story*

# November 29

*Behold, this is our God; we have waited for Him, and He will save us.*

ISAIAH 25:9

When people don't listen, remember Jesus. When tears come, remember Jesus. When disappointment is your bed partner; remember Jesus. When fear pitches his tent in your front yard. When death looms, when anger simmers, when shame weighs heavily. Remember Jesus.

Remember the dead called from the grave with a Galilean accent. Remember the eyes of God that wept human tears.

— MAX LUCADO
*Six Hours, One Day*

# February 1

*You will show me the path of life; in Your presence is fullness of joy; at Your right hand are pleasures forevermore.*

PSALM 16:11

Christ was the most balanced and perhaps the most beloved being ever to enter the society of men. Not only was He gentle and tender and true but also righteous, stern as steel, and terribly tough on phony people.

He was magnificent in His magnanimous spirit of forgiveness for fallen folk but a terror to those who indulged in double talk or false pretenses.

He came to set men free from their own sins, their own selves, their own fears. Those so liberated loved Him with fierce loyalty.

—PHILLIP KELLER
*A Shepherd Looks at Psalm 23*

# November 28

*Light is sown for the righteous, and gladness for the upright in heart.*

PSALM 97:11

God's light pours down over us, even in the darkness. It illuminates the thoughts of our minds, the emotions of the heart. It brightens our pathway.

God sows the light of His Word in our souls as a farmer sows seeds in the ground. The seeds take root, send out tender shoots, grow strong and green and fresh, and ultimately provide fruit.

—PETER WALLACE
*What the Psalmist Is Saying to You*

# February 2

*Faith comes by hearing, and hearing by the word of God.*

ROMANS 10:17

Why would Bible reading produce faith?

Certainly not because there is something magical about the book. The real reasons are far more direct: 1) We can scarcely claim God's promises for ourselves until we know what He has promised. (2) The Bible is a series of true stories of God's dealing with men and women quite like us.

There are pioneers, adventurers, and businessmen.... When we read this book intelligently, we learn how God deals with humankind, what He is like, and what we can expect from Him.

— CATHERINE MARSHALL
*Moments that Matter*

# November 27

*You are my hiding place and my shield; I hope in Your word.*

PSALM 119:114

I firmly believe God's Word has been preserved, not merely as a collection of historical documents and geographical studies, but as a trustworthy resource—a place we turn to for assistance in living our lives in ways that honor Christ.

In the pages of Scripture, God has given us models—people, believe it or not, who are just like you and me, who, despite the odds, lived lives pleasing to Him. By faith. In obedience.

With courage.

— CHARLES R. SWINDOLL
*Paul: A Man of Grace and Grit*

*Casting all your care upon Him, for He cares for you.*
I PETER 5:7

To know God, or even to begin to know Him, is to know that we are not alone in the universe. Someone Else is Out There. There is a hint that there may be a refuge for our loneliness. To stop our frantic getting, spending, and searching, and simply to *look* at the things God has made is to move one step away from despair, for God cares. The most awesome seascape can reveal a care that is actually *tender*.

—ELISABETH ELLIOT
*The Path of Loneliness*

# November 26

*How precious also are Your thoughts to me, O God!*
*How great is the sum of them!*

PSALM 139:17

When I itch for heaven I find that what I really want there is the fulfillment of all that is good about life now—but with its beauty never blotched with ugliness, its pleasure never choked by pain, its plenty never mocked by unfairness to others, its truth never hid by falsehood, its goodness never compromised by evil-and the discovery every day anew that our very beings are alive with God. In short, total fulfillment. Which is, I suppose, what we want when we want heaven.

—LEWIS SMEDES
*Keeping Hope Alive*

# February 4

*It is God who works in you both to will and to do for His good pleasure.*

PHILIPPIANS 2:13

The only purpose or intention God ever has is altogether good. When the Bible speaks of the sovereign exercise of the pleasure of His will, there is no hint of arbitrariness or wicked intent. The pleasure of His will is always the good pleasure of His will. His pleasure is always good; His will is always good; His intentions are always good.

— R. C. SPROUL
*In the Presence of God*

# November 25

*We, according to His promise, look for new heavens and a new earth in which righteousness dwells.*

II PETER 3:13

If God could make the heavens and earth as beautiful as we think they are today—which includes thousands of years of wear and tear, corruption and pollution, sin and selfishness—can you imagine what the new Heaven and the new earth will look like?

—ANNE GRAHAM LOTZ
*Heaven: My Father's House*

# February 5

*He Himself is our peace...and has destroyed the barrier,*
*the dividing wall of hostility.*

EPHESIANS 2:14 NIV

We are guilty and He is innocent.

We are filthy and He is pure.

We are wrong and He is right.

He is not on that cross for His sins. He is there for ours.

—MAX LUCADO
*Six Hours One Friday*

# November 24

*You were not redeemed with corruptible things, like silver
or gold...but with the precious blood of Christ.*

I PETER 1:18-19

We are free either to love God or not. He invites us to love Him. He urges us to love Him. He came that we might love Him. But, in the end, the choice is yours and mine. To take that choice from each of us, for Him to force us to love Him, would be less than love.

God explains the benefits, outlines the promises, and articulates very clearly the consequences. And then, in the end, He leaves the choice to us.

— MAX LUCADO
*And the Angels were Silent*

# February 6

*The Lord is my rock and my fortress and my deliverer;*
*my God, my strength, in whom I will trust.*

PSALM 18:2

God is strong. Solid as a rock. Protective as a fortress and a shield. He is your place of shelter.

His strength is perfect and complete. It's a resource that cannot be exhausted. And it's available to you. So whenever you feel absolutely weak and defeated, vulnerable to sin or depression or failure, draw on His strength. Run to Him.

— PETER WALLACE
*What the Psalmist Is Saying to You*

# *November 23*

*Through wisdom a house is built,...by knowledge the rooms are filled.*
PROVERBS 24:3-4

You may be one who lives your life pursuing fame and fortune, depending on the applause of others. Bad plan. To begin with, fortune has shallow rules. The winds of adversity can quickly blow it all away. Fame is as fickle as the last response from the crowd. Learn a dual lesson. When you're praised and applauded, don't pay any attention. When you're rejected and abused, don't quit.

—*CHARLES R. SWINDOLL*
*Paul: A Man of Grace and Grit*

*February 7*

*I will heal them and reveal to them the abundance of peace and truth.*

JEREMIAH 33:6

God caused the Bible to be written for the express purpose of revealing to man God's plan for redemption. God caused this Book to be written that He might make His everlasting laws clear to His children, and that they might have His great wisdom to guide them and His great love to comfort them as they make their way through life. For without the Bible, this world would indeed be a dark and frightening place, without signpost or beacon.

—BILLY GRAHAM
*Peace with God*

# November 22

*Blessed is the man [whose] delight is in the law of the Lord.*

PSALM 1:1-2

To delight in God's truth means we take time daily to read the Word and meditate on it, and to rejoice when He speaks to us from the sacred page, teaching us a new truth or giving us a new application of a familiar truth.

But the important thing is that we see God and hear His voice as we read His Word. It isn't enough merely to know the truth of God in a doctrinal way; we must also know the God of truth in a personal way.

—WARREN W. WIERSEBE
*The Twenty Essential Qualities*

# February 8

*Humble yourselves in the presence of the Lord, and He will exalt you.*
JAMES 4:10 NASB

God can use our authority and our abundance and our promotion. But before He can, we need to humble ourselves before God's mighty hand and say, "Jesus Christ, I need You. I have all of this to account for, and I can't take any of it with me. Please use me as You see fit." With authority comes the need for accountability. With popularity comes the need for humility. With prosperity comes the need for integrity.

*—CHARLES R. SWINDOLL*
*Joseph*

# November 21

*It is God who works in you both to will and to do for His good pleasure.*

PHILIPPIANS 2:13

It is utterly absurd to assume or suppose that a person who is determined to do his own will can ever please God. Only as our wills are brought into harmony and submission to His will do we discover the secret of divine power and productivity.

One short sentence sums up this whole subject: "Not my will, but Thine be done."

—PHILLIP KELLER

*A Gardener Looks at the Fruits of the Spirit*

# February 9

*The hope of the righteous will be gladness.*

PROVERBS 10:28

One of the great themes of Christianity is triumphant hope. Not just hope as in a distant, vague dream, but *triumphant* hope, the land of hope where all things end right. In the midst of the struggles and the storms and the sufferings of life, we can advance our thoughts beyond today and see relief…triumph…victory. Because, in the end, God does indeed win.

— *CHARLES R. SWINDOLL*

*Esther*

# November 20

*Be ready, for the Son of Man is coming at an hour you do not expect.*

MATTHEW 24:44

Every person who has ever lived will be present at that final gathering. Every heart that has ever beat. Every mouth that has ever spoken. On that day you will be surrounded by a sea of people. Rich, poor. Famous, unknown. Kings, bums.

Brilliant, demented. All will be present. And all will be looking in one direction. All will be looking at Him—the Son of Man. Wrapped in splendor. Shot through with radiance.

—MAX LUCADO
*And the Angels were Silent*

# February 10

*I did not come to judge the world but to save the world.*

JOHN 12:47

We'll often notice things wrong with people, but does that initial look lead to compassion and helping, or to judging and distance? Compassion and judging are two different ways of "seeing."

When we stop judging, we rest from the incessant work of analyzing others. We don't need to figure out what's wrong with people—that's God's job. Our job is to try to understand.

*—PAUL E. MILLER*
*Love Walked Among Us*

# November 19

*He will not allow your foot to be moved; He who keeps you will not slumber.*

PSALM 121:3

The Lord is a personal God, not limited by time or space, One who inhabits the hearts of all who believe in Him. Therefore, no temple or building can contain His presence because He is eternally present throughout the universe.

Have you ever thought that God is with you in all you do and say throughout the day? He is not just present in the morning when you awake. He is with you in the grocery store, in the doctor's office, at work, even at play. No matter where you go, God goes with you.

— *CHARLES STANLEY*
*Into His Presence*

# February 11

*The Lord is good; His mercy is everlasting,
and His truth endures to all generations.*

PSALM 100:5

Truth is timeless. Truth does not differ from one age to another, from one people to another, from one geographical location to another. Men's ideas may differ, men's customs may change, men's moral codes may vary, but God's great all-prevailing Truth stands for time and eternity.

— *BILLY GRAHAM*
*Peace with God*

# November 18

*Let your light so shine before men, that they may see your good works and glorify your Father in heaven.*

MATTHEW 5:16

To the watching world, our lives paint a portrait of God. Our responses to times of gladness and sorrow are like paintbrushes sweeping across the canvas of life, leaving impressions of the God we call Savior. Through our actions and attitudes seekers gather information about this Jesus we proclaim.

With the help of the Holy Spirit, may our lives paint a picture of our God who is...patient but not passive...accepting but not pliable...holy but not untouchable...near but not us.

—ALICIA BRITT CHOLE

*Pure Joy*

# February 12

*The Lord is their strength, and He is the saving refuge of His anointed.*

PSALM 28:8

Once we give ourselves up to God, shall we attempt to get hold of what can never belong to us—*tomorrow?* Our lives are His, our times in His hand. He is Lord over what will happen, never mind what may happen. When we prayed "Thy will be done," did we suppose He did not hear us?

He heard indeed, and daily makes our business His. If my life is once surrendered, all is well. Let me not grab it back, as though it were in peril in His hand but would be safer in mine!

—ELISABETH ELLIOT
*Keep a Quiet Heart*

# November 17

*Love your enemies, do good,...and your reward will be great.*

LUKE 6:35

We may be tempted sometimes to conclude that because God doesn't fix our problem He doesn't love us. There are many things that He does not fix precisely *because* He *loves us.* Instead of extracting us from the problem, He calls us. In our sorrow or loneliness or pain He calls—"This is a necessary part of the journey. *Even* if it is the roughest part, it is only a part, and it will not last the whole long way. Remember where I am leading you. Remember what you will find at the end—a home and a haven and a heaven."

—ELISABETH ELLIOT
*The Path of Loneliness*

# February 13

*The Lord gives wisdom; from His mouth come knowledge and understanding.*

PROVERBS 2:6

God alone is wise. He makes His wisdom available to you, but you must first want it…feel a need of it…yes, REQUIRE, it as essential in your life. Then, and only then, are you putting yourself in a position to partake of God's wisdom and become wise.

—*LARRY LEA*

*Wisdom: The Gift Worth Seeking*

# November 16

*I bow my knees to the Father of our Lord Jesus Christ, from whom the whole family in heaven and earth is named.*

EPHESIANS 3:14-15

You've seen people treat this world like it was a permanent home. It's not. You've seen people pour time and energy into life like it will last forever. It won't. You've seen people so proud of what they have done, that they hope they will never have to leave—they will. We all will. We are in transit. Someday the plane will stop and the deboarding will begin. Wise are those who are ready when the pilot says to get off.

—MAX LUCADO

*And the Angels were Silent*

# February 14

*Whatever God does, it shall be forever.*

ECCLESIASTES 3:14

Though God's people often forgot their God, God didn't forget them. He kept His word. The land became theirs.

When Joseph was dropped into a pit by his own brothers, God didn't give up. When Moses said, "Here I am, send Aaron;" God didn't give up.... When Peter worshiped Him at the supper and cursed Him at the fire, He didn't give up. God never gives up.

— *MAX LUCADO*

*Six Hours One Friday*

# November 15

*He who follows righteousness and mercy finds life, righteousness and honor.*

PROVERBS 21:21

Wisdom isn't for heaven. It's for NOW, *on* this earth.

Wisdom isn't just for the knowing. It's for the doing.

Wisdom isn't for your mind. It's for your hands and feet to implement.

God imparts wisdom to you so you can make a difference in this world… so you can extend His kingdom…so you can enter into the fullness of His blessings for you.

—*LARRY LEA*

*Wisdom: The Gift Worth Seeking*

# February 15

*He who has begun a good work in you*
*will complete it until the day of Jesus Christ.*

PHILIPPIANS 1:6

God is looking for those who believe that what He says is more important than what anyone else says. That what He thinks is more important than what anyone else thinks. That what He wants is more important than what anyone else wants.

That His will is more important than their own.

God is looking for another Noah. Another Meshach. Another Shadrach. Another Abednego.

One person with God is not alone but a majority!

— ANNE GRAHAM LOTZ
*God's Story*

# November 14

*In My Father's house are many mansions.*

JOHN 14:2

Heaven is a big place! "In my Father's house are many mansions"—room enough for anyone and everyone who chooses to be a member of God's family! So please feel free to invite your entire family—including in-laws and out-laws, every one of your friends, all of your neighbors, the total population of your city, your state, your nation—everybody in the whole wide world!

—*ANNE GRAHAM LOTZ*
*Heaven: My Father's House*

# February 16

*God will wipe away every tear from their eyes; there shall*
*be no more death, nor sorrow, nor crying.*

REVELATION 21:4

Christians celebrate the death of Jesus in the Lord's Supper to remember that He died on the cross for the sins of the world. But the supper does not end with the recollection of suffering. We listen to the Lord telling His disciples to repeat this same memorial until He returns. Listening, we rekindle our hope that He will indeed return and that, when He does, God will make His world work right again for everyone.

—LEWIS SMEDES
*Keeping Hope Alive*

# November 13

*Come to Me, all you who labor and are heavy laden, and I will give you rest.*

MATTHEW 11:28

God is an inviting God. He invited Mary to birth His Son, the disciples to fish for men, the adulteress woman to start over, and Thomas to touch His wounds. God is the King who prepares the palace, sets the table, and invites His subjects to come in.

God is a God who invites. God is a God who calls.

— MAX LUCADO

*And the Angels Were Silent*

# February 17

*God is greater than our heart, and knows all things.*

I JOHN 3:20

You and I are governed. The weather determines what we wear. The terrain tells us how to travel. Gravity dictates our speed, and health determines our strength. We may challenge these forces and alter them slightly, but we never remove them.

God—our Shepherd—doesn't check the weather; He makes it. He doesn't defy gravity; He created it.

God is what He is. What He has always been. God is Yahweh—an unchanging God, an uncaused God, and an ungoverned God.

*—MAX LUCADO*
*Traveling Light*

# November 12

*My God shall supply all your need according
to His riches in glory by Christ Jesus.*

PHILIPPIANS 4:19

God is in control. When a job is terminated, a mate quits, a friend deserts, God is quietly but sovereignly at work for your good. You are not a victim of the economy or another's decision.

You can be content in any circumstance when you are sure of God's unceasing care and absolute control over every detail. Rest in His ability, and contentment will follow.

—CHARLES STANLEY
*Into His Presence*

# February 18

*Teach us to number our days, that we may gain a heart of wisdom.*

PSALM 90:12

In very truth I have only today. Yesterday is gone forever. There is no guarantee I shall be here tomorrow. So in reality I am locked into a single *day-tight* time and space concept. I have the choke—either I can worry my way through it or I can revel and rejoice in this interval of time provided by my Father.

—*PHILLIP KELLER*

*A Gardener Looks at the Fruits of the Spirit*

# November 11

*Count it all joy when you fall into various trials, knowing that the testing of your faith produces patience.*

JAMES 1:2

Trials, James tells us, prove the authenticity of our faith.

Truth is, we would rather be perfected and completed by viewing a motivational video, attending a challenging conference, reading an inspiring book. (about someone else who went through trials), or… anything but testing!…

We long for controlled, comfortable, circumstances. But pure JOY is the fruit of tested, patient, faith.

—*ALICIA BRITT CHOLE*
*Pure Joy*

# *February 19*

*You are my lamp, O Lord; the Lord shall enlighten my darkness.*

II SAMUEL 22:29

Knowledge of the Bible is essential to a rich and meaningful life, for the words of this Book have a way of filling in the missing pieces, of bridging the gaps, of turning the tarnished colors of our life to jewel-like brilliance. Learn to take your every problem to the Bible. Within its pages you will find the correct answer.

—*BILLY GRAHAM*
*Peace with God*

# November 10

*The Lord will perfect that which concerns me;*
*Your mercy, O Lord, endures forever.*

PSALM 138:8

To magnify something, you make it look larger, increasing it out of proportion. To talk about ourselves or our activities out of true proportion is dangerous indeed, but when we magnify God, we are on safe ground. We simply cannot say too much about God's goodness or love. The most exaggerated things we can think of will still be far below what is actually the case.

—RICHARD FOSTER
*Prayer: Finding the Head's True Home*

# February 20

*You are My friends if you do whatever I command you.*

JOHN 15:14

There are no miseries in heaven. There is no hardship or pain in heaven. Only contentment, and joy, and perfect peace. When you enjoy doing the will of God, you are bringing heaven into your heart. Do you want a piece of heaven on earth? Obey the will of God.

—MICHAEL YOUSSEF

*The Prayer That God Answers*

# November 9

*Now abide faith, hope, love, these three; but the greatest of these is love.*

I CORINTHIANS 13:13

Paul not only distinguishes among faith, hope, and love, but also links them to show that they remain connected and mutually dependent on each other. The biblical concept of hope does not lack the confidence that our cultural concept of hope does.

Rather, hope is faith looking forward to the future. It is a hope that will not disappoint or leave us ashamed.

—R. C. SPROUL
*Loved By God*

# February 21

*I have come that they may have life, and that they may have it more abundantly.*

JOHN 10:10

In the cross, the Lord God arranged a plan for our spiritual survival with divine integrity. It required the sacrifice of Christ on the cross. He followed through. We can take Him at His word. He was who He said He was, and He did what He said He would do. With a single heart and a single mind and a single will, He fulfilled the Father's plan.

— CHARLES R. SWINDOLL

*Joseph*

*Though He was rich, yet for your sakes He became poor,
that you through His poverty might become rich.*

II CORINTHIANS 8:9

During His earthly ministry, Jesus not only shared precious gifts with needy people—sight to the blind, food to the hungry, healing to the sick, even life to the dead—but Jesus gave Himself for all people so that anybody who trusted Him would share the riches of His grace. Furthermore, He didn't simply take away the bad and replace it with the good, Jesus took on Himself all that was bad in us, including our sins, so that He might share with us all the good that is in Him.

—WARREN W. WIERSEBE
*The Twenty Essential Qualities*

# February 22

*He who heeds the word wisely will find good, and*
*whoever trusts in the Lord, happy is he.*

PROVERBS 16:20

When you find yourself drowning in overwhelming circumstances, ask God to give you a promise to which you can cling—promise on which you can base your hope. Hope that is based simply on what you want or what you feel is not a genuine expression of faith. Our hope must be based on God's word.

—ANNE GRAHAM LOTZ
*God's Story*

# November 7

*I do not seek My own will but the will of the Father who sent Me.*

JOHN 5:30

Wherever Christ moved, whomever He met, whatever circumstances He encountered, the remarkable aspect of His life was that He was always in control. He was never taken unawares, never caught in a crisis. Jesus was never manipulated, nor was He ever at the mercy of the mob.

Jesus of Nazareth, the Christ of God, was supremely in control. And this was because He was God-controlled.

—PHILLIP KELLER

*A Gardener Looks at the Fruits of the Spirit*

*He makes me to lie down in green pastures; He leads me beside the still waters.*

PSALM 23:2

Note the two pronouns preceding the two verbs. He makes me…
He leads me…

Who is in charge? The shepherd. The shepherd selects the trail and prepares the pasture. The sheep's job—our job—is to watch the shepherd.

—*MAX LUCADO*
*Traveling Light*

# November 6

*Truly our fellowship is with the Father and with His Son Jesus Christ.*

I JOHN 1:3

Jesus had a humble heart. If He abides in us, pride will never dominate our lives. Jesus had a loving heart. If He dwells within us, hatred and bitterness will never rule us. Jesus had a forgiving and understanding heart. If He lives within us, mercy will temper our relationships with our fellowmen.

—BILLY GRAHAM
*The Secret of Happiness*

# February 24

*He will be very gracious to you at the sound of your cry; when He hears it, He will answer you.*

ISAIAH 30:19

Be specific in your prayer life. If you need a job, pray for a job. If you're an engineer, ask God to open up an engineering position for you, or something related for which you are qualified….

If you need fifteen hundred dollars for tuition, ask for that amount. Make your petitions specific.

— CHARLES R. SWINDOLL
*Elijah*

# November 5

*I delight to do Your will, O my God, and Your law is within my heart.*

PSALM 40:8

The situation that looms in front of you may seem impossible to overcome in your own strength. It might be the result of your own actions, or you may be an innocent victim, caught in the backlash of someone else's consequences. Whatever the case, we can easily become intimidated, even fearful, and eventually immobile. The only way to move beyond that sort of paralyzing stalemate is to learn to accept and trust God's plan. You release the controls and wait for Him to move.

— CHARLES R. SWINDOLL
*Paul: A Man of Grace and Grit*

*I will wait for the God of my salvation; my God will hear me.*
MICAH 7:7

Even in the Garden of Gethsemane on the night of betrayal, Christ had plenty of time and opportunity to flee.

But He would not flee. Instead He knelt to pray in the shadowy Garden under the gray-green leaves of the olive trees. And in His prayer that night, Jesus gave us, for all time, the perfect pattern for the Prayer of Relinquishment: "Not what I want, but what You want."…Jesus deliberately set Himself to make His will and God's will the same.

— CATHERINE MARSHALL
*Moments that Matter*

# November 4

*You have always been, and You will always be. To You,*
*a thousand years is like the passing of a day.*

PSALM 90:2,4 NCV

God is intimately involved in every nanosecond of every moment of
every day in every life. Even when the time of your life seems totally
out of control, speeding and changing so that you can barely catch your
breath, He is behind every tick of the clock. And when life slows down to a
crawl through boredom or depression, He still holds you firm in His sight.

—PETER WALLACE
*What the Psalmist Is Saying to You*

# February 26

*Your thoughts toward us cannot be recounted to You in order; if I would declare and speak of them, they are more than can be numbered.*

PSALM 40:5

As a watch must have a designer, so our precision-like universe has a Great Designer. We call Him God. His is a name with which we are familiar. From earliest childhood we have breathed His name. The Bible declares that the God we talk about, the God we sing about, the God "from whom all blessing flow!" is the God who created this world and placed us in it.

—BILLY GRAHAM
*Peace with God*

# November 3

*The Lord Himself will come down from heaven, with a loud command.*

I THESSALONIANS 4:16 NIV

Have you ever wondered what that command will be? It will be the inaugural word of heaven.

I could very well be wrong, but I think the command that puts an end to the pains of the earth and initiates the joys of heaven will be two words: "No more."

No more loneliness. No more tears. No more death. No more sadness. No more crying. No more pain.

—MAX LUCADO

*And the Angels were Silent*

# February 27

*Behold, God is my salvation, I will trust and not be afraid.*

ISAIAH 12:2

God deals with the hard questions of life. Not questions like how do I make a living, but how do I make a life? Not how do I spend my time, but how do I spend eternity? And not so much how do I get along with the person who sits next to me, but ultimately, how do I get along with God? When we answer the hard questions correctly, all the others fall into place.

— CHARLES R. SWINDOLL

*Joseph*

# November 2

*Greater love has no one than this, than to lay down one's life for his friends.*

JOHN 15:13

The only crown Jesus ever wore on earth was a crown of thorns.

What does that crown tell us about the love of God the Father? Much every way. For one thing, it tells us that His love is not a sentimental thing, for it was strong enough to hurt His own Son. He could have rescued Him with "legions of angels." He did not do so.

What does the crown of thorns tell us about the love of God the Son? It tells us that it was strong enough to deny itself, strong enough to suffer.

— ELISABETH ELLIOT
*The Path of Loneliness*

# February 28

*[He] is able to do exceedingly abundantly above all that we ask or think.*

EPHESIANS 3:20

Instead of raging against the Lord for the way He manages our lives, let us carefully consider all the benefits He bestows. Take a piece of paper; sit down alone in a quiet spot; write down one by one all the good things—the delights and the pleasures He has made possible for you. List everything—the sound of music; the laughter of children; the sunrise; the scent of a rose; the clasp of a friend's hand; the loyalty of a dog. If one is honest, there is no end to the list.

—PHILLIP KELLER
*A Gardener Looks at the Fruits of the Spirit*

# November 1

*As for God, His way is perfect.*

PSALM 18:30

Is anyone perfect? No, not anyone on earth. Only God is perfect! And you don't need to be God—not in your own appraisal of yourself or in relation to anybody. You are free to simply be you.

There will always be aspects of you that fall short of some idealized goal. As you are able to recognize and accept these aspects, you will have a chance to modify them and improve them. And you will set other people free to do the same.

—NEIL CLARK WARREN
*God Said It, Don't Sweat It*

## February 29

*He who promised is faithful.*

HEBREWS 10:23

A strong faith leads to a good attitude.

— CHARLES R. SWINDOLL

## October 31

*Trust in the Lord and do good.*

PSALM 37:3

If you wish to be a man or woman of God who desires to live a godly life that will leave its mark upon this world, you must stand in the shadow of your Savior. Trust Him to work through the trials you encounter, through the extreme circumstances you cannot handle on your own. He is still the God of impossible situations. He does what no earthly individual can do.

*—CHARLES R. SWINDOLL*
*Day by Day*

# *March 1*

*Godliness with contentment is great gain.*

I TIMOTHY 6:6

When we surrender to God the cumbersome sack of discontent, we don't just give up something; we gain something. God replaces it with a lightweight, tailor-made, sorrow-resistant attaché of gratitude.

What will you gain with contentment? You may gain your marriage. You may gain precious hours with your children. You may gain your self-respect. You may gain joy.

—*MAX LUCADO*
*Traveling Light*

# *October 30*

*The fear of the Lord leads to life, and he who has it will abide in satisfaction.*

PROVERBS 19:23

Sometimes the wisdom of God will be a bitter herb to you. It will be contrary to the way you want to do things or the way you want to experience life. But if you will swallow that bitter pill or, in other words, go ahead and DO what you know to do, no matter how hard it is and no matter how much you have to ENDURE—then you'll find yourself in a position to be resurrected by God with great victory!

—*LARRY LEA*
*Wisdom: The Gift Worth Seeking*

# March 2

*You are a chosen generation, a royal priesthood,…the people of God.*

I PETER 2:9-10

Several images are used in the Bible to describe the Church: the Body of Christ, the elect, the house of God, the saints. One of the most meaningful expressions the Bible uses is "the people of God," the *laos theon.*

The Church is not a building; it is not the clergy; it is not an abstract institution—it is the people of God.

— R. C. SPROUL
*In the Presence of God*

## October 29

*Commit your way to the Lord, trust also in Him, and He shall bring it to pass.*

PSALM 37:5

Acceptance of discipleship is the utter abandonment of the disciple, the surrender of all rights, to the Master. This abandonment, in all cases, will mean pain. Christ listed some of the troubles His followers could expect, so they would not be taken by surprise and thus discard their faith in Him. He did not offer immunity. He asked for trust.

—*ELISABETH ELLIOT*
*The Path of Loneliness*

# March 3

*It is God who arms me with strength, and makes my way perfect.*

PSALM 18:32

Who is God? He is the Lord. He is the Sovereign Ruler of the universe. He is intimately involved in your life. He knows what you're feeling and why. He knows what you need, and He will give it as you can receive it.

He is a rock-strong, bold, mighty, immovable, unyielding in power.

The Lord your God will guide you right.

—PETER WALLACE
*What the Psalmist Is Saying to You*

# October 28

*Delight yourself also in the Lord, and He shall give you the desires of your heart.*

PSALM 37:4

This promise is not carte blanche to get what we want from God just because we belong to His family. David is saying that, if we truly delight in the Lord, we will want to know Him. better; and the better we know Him, the more we will become like Him. *His* desires will become *our* desires, and our greatest desires will be to know Him *even* more and enjoy Him in an ever-deepening way.

—WARREN W. WIERSEBE
*The Twenty Essential Qualities*

# *March 4*

*Take my yoke upon you and learn from Me…*
*and you will find rest for your souls.*

MATTHEW 11:29

Discipleship is the call to Calvary, first and foremost to receive the forgiveness and salvation provided by God's great love. But we are never to remain solely as forgiven penitents. We are called to grow as God's sons and daughters, to serve as His faithful stewards, to learn as His devoted disciples. And all of that growth, service, and learning is most practically processed not by the way we handle life's blessings, but by the way we live through its bad days.

*—JACK HAYFORD*
*How to Live Through a Bad Day*

# October 27

*The person who continues to be strong until the end will be saved.*
MATTHEW 24:13 NCV

The Brazilians have a great phrase for this. In Portuguese, a person who has the ability to hang in and not give up has *garra*. *Garra* means "claws." What imagery! A person with *garra* has claws which burrow in the side of the cliff and keep him from falling.

So do the saved. They may get close to the edge. They may even stumble and slide. But they will dig their nails into the rock of God and hang on.

—MAX LUCADO
*And the Angels were Silent*

# March 5

*Every word of God is pure; He is a shield to those who put their trust in Him.*

PROVERBS 30:5

God has not changed. If He was faithful to watch over Noah and all those within the ark, bringing them safely through the storm, He will do the same for you. Just as He was faithful to preserve Joseph through thirteen years of slavery in Potiphar's house and Pharaoh's prison, just as He was faithful to preserve the little baby Moses floating on the Nile…God will be faithful to you.

—ANNE GRAHAM LOTZ
*God's Story*

## October 26

*We have a building from God, a house*
*not made with hands, eternal in the heavens.*

II CORINTHIANS 5:5

Earth's heartaches are healed by the promises of God. When we are home at last, the homesickness will be over. We shall praise the King who knew how to cut eternal doorways in mere holes cut in sod. Joy belongs to all those who understand that earth is but a rehearsal for heaven.

On dim evenings, if you squint at sunsets, you can all but see the promise. In our Father's house there really are many mansions—and one of them is ours.

— CALVIN MILLER
*Into the Depths of God*

# March 6

*Blessed are those who keep justice, and he who does righteousness at all times!*

PSALM 106:3

We rejoice over each day we can live for God. We give hearty and humble thanks for His abundant and gracious care, living in a constant "attitude of gratitude." To live this way is to live out in the open sunlight of His presence. It is to live in honest dignity and strength and serene simplicity. It is to live above the clutter and complications of a complex society that would crowd and choke out our fruitfulness for God.

—PHILLIP KELLER

*A Gardener Looks at the Fruits of the Spirit*

# October 25

*As the heavens are high above the earth, so great is*
*His mercy toward those who fear Him.*

PSALM 103:11

A dversity can be handled one of two ways. Either you can deal with it on your own, or you can allow God to carry your burden for you. The first requires human strength and effort, which are rarely sufficient in handling grievous trials. Heartache erodes human ability.

The wiser course of action is to allow God to handle your adversity. His ability to provide goes beyond our greatest imagination. He is the God who has the ability to calm every storm.

— CHARLES STANLEY
*Into His Presence*

# March 7

*God's business is putting things right; He loves getting the lines straight.*
PSALM 11:7 THE MESSAGE

In the wilderness of loneliness we are terribly vulnerable. What we want is OUT, and sometimes there appear to be some easy ways to get there. Will we take Satan up on his offers, satisfy our desires in ways never designed by God, seek security outside of His holy will? If we do, we may find a measure of happiness, but not the lasting joy our heavenly Father wants us to have.

—ELISABETH ELLIOT
*The Path of Loneliness*

# October 24

*The Lord is near to those who have a broken heart,*
*and saves such as have a contrite spirit.*

PSALM 34:18

In brokenness and contrition the humbled person cries out to God for help. He reaches out to Christ for restoration and healing. He exercises faith in another because he knows he must touch someone greater than himself. Similarly he seeks out others he can serve and in his suffering service finds fulfillment and freedom from himself. It is to such souls that God gives Himself gladly, freely.

—PHILLIP KELLER
*A Gardener Looks at the Fruits of the Spirit*

# March 8

*Walk in love, as Christ also has loved us and given Himself for us.*

EPHESIANS 5:2

Do you love others? Do you love others as you love yourself? If so, you are undoubtedly in a right relationship with God! But if you find yourself focusing all of your attention on your own life exclusive of others, you can know for a fact that you haven't loved yourself the way you need to. All the love you need is totally available to you right now! God is ready to love you so powerfully that your love for others will become automatic and natural.

—NEIL CLARK WARREN
*God Said It, Don't Sweat It*

# October 23

*He who is spiritual judges all things, yet He Himself is rightly judged by no one.*

I CORINTHIANS 2:15

God defines the spiritual person as one who judges all things. This means that the truly spiritual person is capable of discerning between natural wisdom and spiritual wisdom. The truly spiritual person is able to discern what God is truly saying about a matter and then acts on it.

Our challenge is to...decide it is God's answers and God's solutions that we truly want in our lives.

—LARRY LEA
*Wisdom: The Gift Worth Seeking*

## March 9

*This is the victory that has overcome the world—our faith.*

I JOHN 5:4

There is a difference between acceptance and resignation.

Resignation is barren of faith in the love of God. It says, "Grievous circumstances have come to me. There is no escaping them."

Acceptance says, "I trust the goodwill, the love of my God. I'll open my arms and my understanding to what He has allowed to come to me." Thus acceptance leaves the door of hope wide open to God's creative plan.

— *CATHERINE MARSHALL*
*Moments that Matter*

## October 22

*It is finished!*
JOHN 19:30

The dawn of world redemption had broken, and with it the chains of human slavery to sin, shame, and condemnation were being shattered.

"It is finished!" was the Son of God's invitation to join Him in the conviction that now—because of the cross—there is nothing we struggle with that is without either a purpose or an end. No struggle need ever be pointless. No suffering need ever be unending.

—*JACK HAYFORD*
*How to Live Through a Bad Day*

# March 10

*[God] is right in everything he does.*
DANIEL 9:14 NCV

God is never wrong. He has never rendered a wrong decision, experienced the wrong attitude, taken the wrong path, said the wrong thing, or acted the wrong way. He is never too late or too early, too loud or too soft, too fast or too slow. He has always been and always will be right.

He is righteous.

—MAX LUCADO
*Traveling Light*

# October 21

*He will speak peace to His people and to His saints.*

PSALM 85:8

If God says, "I forgive you," who are you to say, "Thank You, God, but I can't forgive myself"? Are your standards higher than His? Are you more righteous than He is? If God says, "I forgive you," then the only appropriate response is to say, "God, thank You. I don't deserve it, but I accept it. And to express my gratitude, I, in turn, forgive that person who has sinned against me."

—ANNE GRAHAM LOTZ
*Just Give Me Jesus*

# March 11

*He who believes in the Son of God has the witness in himself.*

I JOHN 5:10

**M**an's only salvation from sin stands on a lonely, barren, skull-shaped hill; a thief hangs on one cross, a murderer on another, and between them, a Man with a crown of thorns. Blood flows from His hands and feet, it pours from His side, it drops down His face—while those who stand looking on sneer and mock.

Who is this tortured figure, this Man whom other men seek to humiliate and kill? He is the Son of God, the Prince of Peace.

*— BILLY GRAHAM*
*Peace with God*

*In Your presence is fullness of joy.*

PSALM 16:11

David didn't have an easy life either before or after he became king. He was familiar with false accusation, homelessness, failure, betrayal, and family strife. Yet his psalms are filled with expressions of joy.

In spite of circumstances, David chose joy. He could have chosen pity, anger, loneliness, frustration, or fear. He chose joy.

— ALICIA BRITT CHOLE

*Pure Joy*

# March 12

*The fear of the Lord is the beginning of wisdom.*

PSALM 111:10

Persons who fear the Lord are persons who can hardly wait to do the commandments of God. They are a delight, not a chore. They are exciting, not boring. They are thrilling, not devastating. When God says something to persons who fear the Lord, they are EAGER to jump into action and get the job done! They have a sense of holy excitement.

—*LARRY LEA*

*Wisdom: The Gift Worth Seeking*

# October 19

*Your righteousness is an everlasting righteousness, and Your law is truth.*

PSALM 119:142

Each of us must become as a little child and by faith grasp what we cannot altogether understand. But faith is not a blind leap in the dark! It is instead based squarely on what God has done for us in Jesus Christ. Our faith has a firm foundation, because it is not based on speculation or wishful thinking, but upon God and His Word. God can be trusted to keep His promises to us.

—BILLY GRAHAM
*The Secret of Happiness*

# March 13

*Be kind to one another,…forgiving one another.*

EPHESIANS 4:32

Forgiving is a minor miracle, a bloodless surgery we perform on our spirits. It goes like this, though not necessarily in this order: (1) We begin to see the offender as a…blemished person not all that much different from ourselves. (2) We surrender our precious right to get even… and choose to live with the scales unbalanced. (3) We gradually, oh so gradually, find the will to wish him well.

Once begun—and remember that it is almost always a process, sometimes a lifelong journey—we…have hope again. People who discover the grace to forgive almost always discover the grace of hope besides.

—*LEWIS SMEDES*
*Keeping Hope Alive*

# October 18

*We are in Him who is true, in His Son Jesus Christ.*
I JOHN 5:20

We have been shown the way of acceptance on every page of the life of Jesus. It sprang from love and from trust. He set His face like a flint toward Jerusalem. He took up the Cross of His own will. No one could take His life from Him. He deliberately laid it down. He calls us to take up our crosses. That is a different thing from capitulation or resignation. It is a glad and voluntary YES.

— ELISABETH ELLIOT
*The Path of Loneliness*

# March 14

*Christ died for sins once for all, the righteous for*
*the unrighteous, to bring you to God.*

I PETER 3:18 NIV

The path of righteousness is a narrow, winding trail up a steep hill. At
the top of the hill is a cross. At the base of the cross are bags. Countless
bags full of innumerable sins. Calvary is the compost pile of guilt. Would
you like to leave yours there as well?

—MAX LUCADO
*Traveling Light*

# October 17

*I will be a Father to you, and you shall be My sons*
*and daughters," says the Lord Almighty.*

II CORINTHIANS 6:18

God did what we wouldn't dare dream. He did what we couldn't imagine. He became a man so we could trust Him. He became a sacrifice so we could know Him. And He defeated death so we could follow Him.

It defies logic. It is a divine insanity. Holy incredibility.

Only a Creator beyond the fence of logic could offer such a gift of love.

What man can't do, God does.

— MAX LUCADO
*And the Angels were Silent*

# *March 15*

*The wages of sin is death, but the gift of God*
*is eternal life in Christ Jesus our Lord.*

ROMANS 6:23

The cross, sin's masterpiece of shame and hate, became God's masterpiece of mercy and forgiveness. Through the death of Christ upon the cross, sin itself was crucified for those who believe in Him. Sin was conquered on the cross. His death is the foundation of our hope, the promise of our triumph!

—*BILLY GRAHAM*
*Peace with God*

# October 16

*When my spirit was overwhelmed within me, then You knew my path.*

PSALM 142:3

Hoping in God is hoping when there is no hope. Hoping in God is to trust that He will be there with us when we put our feet in places so godforsaken that He will be there holding us up when we are falling over the edge. Leading us through our private darkness. Being there-ahead of us, behind us, above us, under us, for us, and even *in* us.

—LEWIS SMEDES
*Keeping Hope Alive*

# March 16

*Blessed is that man who makes the Lord his trust.*

PSALM 40:4

When the Israelites left Egypt, they headed across the Red Sea to Mount Sinai. From there it was only about a two-week journey into the promised land. Fourteen days turned into *forty years*. A blind camel would have found its way sooner than that. God designed a supernaturally long trail in order to deal with what was in their hearts.

—JOHN ELDREDGE
*The Journey of Desire*

## October 15

*Be steadfast, immovable, always abounding in the work of the Lord, knowing that your labor is not in vain in the Lord.*

I CORINTHIANS 15:58

One day, God Himself will take your face in His hands and gently wipe away your tears as He reassures you there will be no more suffering. There will be no more broken homes or broken hearts, broken lives or broken dreams.

You can look forward with hope, because one day there will be no more separation, no more scars, and no more suffering in My Father's House. It's the home of your dreams!

—ANNE GRAHAM LOTZ
*Heaven: My Father's House*

# March 17

*The heavens are Yours, the earth also is Yours;…*
*You have a mighty arm; strong is Your hand.*

PSALM 89:11, 13

As you and I see the winter snows give way to spring flowers and the summer's heat give way to autumn's briskness, we are reminded that in back of the changes is the God Who never changes. The sun that always rises every morning and always sets every evening, the stars that always come out in the night sky, and the moon that always goes through its monthly phases—all reveal the glory of God, Who is good!

—ANNE GRAHAM LOTZ
*God's Story*

# October 14

*Those who wait on the Lord shall renew their strength.*

ISAIAH 40:31

I love that verse. The word renew can also be translated as exchanged. In other words, Isaiah said, "Those who wait on the Lord shall exchange their strength for His strength." That's a great exchange, friend! I'd much rather have His strength than my strength any day, any hour, any minute, any second!

—*LARRY LEA*
*Wisdom: The Gift Worth Seeking*

# March 18

*Trust God from the bottom of your heart; don't try
to figure out everything on your own.*

PROVERBS 3:5 THE MESSAGE

Whatever life gives us opportunity to do, let us do it well. Let us do it to the best of our ability, then leave the results with Christ.

It is not for us to decide or determine what the net results of our living will be. It is God who keeps the eternal accounts. Only He can ascertain what is of consequence in His economy.

—PHILLIP KELLER
*A Gardener Looks at the Fruits of the Spirit*

# October 13

*We ought to obey God rather than men.*

ACTS 5:29

If you're getting ready to go off to school or getting ready to launch a new phase of your career, don't do it without first establishing a regular time to meet alone with the Lord.... Your spiritual future depends on it. Without that commitment to saturate your life with God's Word, you step into the unknown future at your own risk.

—CHARLES R. SWINDOLL

*Paul: A Man of Grace and Grit*

# March 19

*There is no fear in love; but perfect love casts out fear.*

I JOHN 4:18

The unconditional love we so desperately need if we are to become authentic comes only from God. Interestingly enough, it is when we let God love us unconditionally at a deep level that we tend to become the person He really wants us to be. It is only when we feel His total love for us that we are free to be genuine in all of our relations with others. This genuineness, I feel confident, is exactly what pleases Him most.

—NEIL CLARK WARREN
*God said It, Don't Sweat It*

# October 12

*Blessed are the pure in heart, for they shall see God.*

MATTHEW 5:8

Jesus said, "Happy are the pure in heart." Now, we should be able to take that for just what it means. If the heart is the seat of affection, then our love toward God must be pure. If the heart is the center of our motives, then our motives must be pure. If the heart is the residence of our wills, then our wills must be yielded to Christ. We are to be pure in love, pure in motive, and pure in desire.

—BILLY GRAHAM
*The Secret of Happiness*

# March 20

*In quietness and confidence shall be your strength.*

ISAIAH 30:15

God never forgets anything He promises. That's right…never.

God's agenda continues to unfold right on schedule, even when there is not a shred of evidence that He remembers. Even when the most extreme events transpire and "life just doesn't seem fair," God is there, carrying out His providential plan exactly as He pre-arranged it. He keeps His word.

— *CHARLES R. SWINDOLL*

*Elijah*

# October 11

*His divine power has given to us all things that pertain to life and godliness, through the knowledge of Him who called us by glory and virtue.*

II PETER 1:3

**M**any believers do not understand the vast riches they already possess in Jesus Christ, an infinite treasury of wisdom and knowledge and all good things. The moment you accept Him as your Savior you receive everything God is, everything God does, and everything God provides. You lack nothing. God's immeasurable, overflowing love and power are available to you by His grace for every trial, every decision, every challenge.

*— CHARLES STANLEY*
*Into His Presence*

# March 21

*A man has joy by the answer of his mouth, and a word
spoken in due season, how good it is!*

PROVERBS 15:23

Mark Twain once said that the difference between the right word and the nearly right word is the difference between lightning and a lightning bug. In other words, it's huge. What we say and don't say… matters.

Words have the power to heal and to hurt. They have the ability to win people over or wound them for years to come. It's very important that we choose our words wisely…. God can help us with that if we ask Him.

—*JOHN HULL AND TIM ELMORE*
*Pivotal Praying*

# October 10

*Great peace have those who love Your law, and nothing causes them to stumble.*

PSALM 119:165

Believers who spend time daily in the Word and prayer gradually develop a spiritual radar, a practical wisdom from the Holy Spirit that gives us direction when we need It. Sometimes that direction comes from a promise or warning in Scripture, sometimes from God's providential working in circumstances, and sometimes from the Spirit's witness in our hearts. Even a chance remark by a friend can be used of God to guide us if our minds and hearts are prepared and we're willing to obey God's leading.

—WARREN W. WIERSEBE
*The Twenty Essential Qualities*

# March 22

*The fear of the Lord is the instruction of wisdom.*

PROVERBS 15:33

Freedom to choose or to reject, freedom to obey God's commands or to go contrary to them, freedom to make himself happy or miserable. For it is not the mere possession of freedom that makes life satisfying—it is what we choose to do with our freedom that determines whether or not we shall find peace with God and with ourselves.

—BILLY GRAHAM
*Peace with God*

# October 9

*This is the love of God, that we keep His commandments.*
*And His commandments are not burdensome.*

I JOHN 5:3

When we awaken in the morning, we choose the attitude that will ultimately guide our thoughts and actions through the day. I'm convinced our best attitudes emerge out of a clear understanding of our own identity, a clear sense of our divine mission, and a deep sense of God's purpose for our lives. That sort of God-honoring attitude encourages us to press on, to focus on the goal, to respond in remarkable ways to life's most extreme circumstances.

— *CHARLES R. SWINDOLL*
*Paul: A Man of Grace and Grit*

# *March 23*

*The cross of our Lord Jesus Christ is my only reason for bragging.*
GALATIANS 6:14 NCV

D o you feel a need for affirmation? Does your self-esteem need attention? You don't need to drop names or show off. You need only pause at the base of the cross and be reminded of this: The maker of the stars would rather die for you than live without you. And that is a fact. So if you need to brag, brag about that.

— MAX LUCADO
*Traveling Light*

# October 8

*He who loves me will be loved by My Father, and I will love him.*
JOHN 14:21

Jesus purposefully pursued *quiet time* with His Father—a sacred space worthy of sacrifice, where the urgent bows to the eternal; a gift—not a waste—of time for God.

Carving out moments to be alone with God is an exercise in stillness where we elevate Creator above creation, "being" above "doing." Where we listen to the One who is always listening to us.

Resting in God's presence, our soul enjoys a banquet from God's Word. Our minds forge an alliance with truth, and dreams are born.

—ALICIA BRITT CHOLE
*Pure Joy*

# March 24

*Hope does not disappoint, because the love of God has been poured out in our hearts by the Holy Spirit who was given to us.*

ROMANS 5:5

Have you become so overwhelmed with your own weakness and failure and sin and inability to live a life that is pleasing to God that you have begun to doubt your salvation? Then look up! Take a good, long look at the cross and remember that God *remembers*. He loves you, He has forgiven you, He is eternally committed to you, and you are saved! Forever! Praise God! His covenant is unconditional!

—ANNE GRAHAM LOTZ
*God's Story*

## October 7

*Since we are receiving a kingdom which cannot be shaken,*
*let us have grace, by which we may serve God.*

HEBREWS 12:28

God is a God who opens the door and waves His hand, pointing pilgrims to a full table. His invitation is not just for a meal, however. It is for life. An invitation to come into His kingdom and take up residence in a tearless, graveless, painless world. Who can come? Whoever wishes. The invitation is at once universal and personal.

—MAX LUCADO
*And the Angels were Silent*

# March 25

*Fear not, for I am with you.*

ISAIAH 41:10

God knows where we are. Sometimes we forget this. Sometimes we even feel that God has forgotten us. He hasn't. God knows exactly where we are. So when you are afflicted with those forsaken feelings, when you're on the verge of throwing a pity party, thanks to those despairing thoughts, go back to the Word of God. God says, "I know where you are."

—*CHARLES R. SWINDOLL*
*Elijah*

# October 6

*In this is love, not that we loved God, but that He loved us
and sent His son to be the propitiation for our sins.*

I JOHN 4:10

In the end, all we've ever really wanted is to be loved. "Love comes from God," writes St. John. We don't have to get God to love us by doing something right—even loving Him. "This is love: not that we loved God but that He loved us and sent His Son as an atoning sacrifice for our sins." Someone has noticed, someone has taken initiative. There is nothing we need to do to keep it up, because His love for us is not based on what we've done, but who we are: His beloved.

— BRENT CURTIS AND JOHN ELDREDGE
*The Sacred Romance*

# March 26

*Because He has set His love upon Me, therefore I will deliver him;*
*I will set him on high, because he has known My name.*

PSALM 91:14

The first step toward God is realizing you are on the wrong path going the wrong way. It's actually quite freeing if you think about it. With your mask off you can get real and relax.

When we realize we don't have it all together, we can care for people because we no longer feel morally superior to them. Consequently, we are quicker to help than to give advice, quicker to listen than to lecture.

—PAUL E. MILLER
*Love Walked Among Us*

## October 5

*If you love Me, keep My commandments.*

JOHN 14:15

The cross is not just a symbol of love or a fashion statement. The cross is your daily decision to deny yourself, your rights, your wants, your dreams, your plans, your goals, and deliberately, wholeheartedly, unreservedly live out your commitment to God's will and God's way and God's Word and God's wisdom. The cross is your decision to live for Him. Period.

—ANNE GRAHAM LOTZ
*Just Give Me Jesus*

# March 27

*He will rejoice over you with gladness, He will quiet you with His love.*
ZEPHANIAH 3:17

What happens when we find ourselves in the kingdom of God? The disabled jump to their feet and start doing a jig. The deaf go out and buy themselves stereo equipment. The blind are headed to the movies. The dead are not dead at all anymore, but very much alive. They show up for dinner. In other words, human brokenness in all its forms is healed. The kingdom of God brings *restoration*.

—JOHN ELDREDGE
*The Journey of Desire*

# October 4

*The Lord God is my strength; He will make my feet like deer's feet, and He will make me walk on my high hills.*

HABAKKUK 3:19

How do you bring yourself to go on when the roof is caving in on you at the same time as the floor is falling out from under you and the walls are crashing in? Is God even there?

Some situations are so complicated and overwhelming that we're tempted to just walk away and quit. However, we need to explore what God's up to and what He's trying to teach us in the midst of tough times. At pivotal moments like these, we shouldn't push away from God, but run to Him in prayer.

—JOHN HULL AND TIM ELMORE
*Pivotal Praying*

# *March 28*

*As the heavens are higher than the earth, so are My ways higher than your ways, and My thoughts than your thoughts.*

ISAIAH 55:9

When we begin praying for others, we soon discover that it is easy to become discouraged at the results, which seem frustratingly slow and uneven. This is because we are entering the strange mix of divine influence and human autonomy.

God never compels…. His way is like the rain and the snow that gently fall to the earth, disappearing into the ground as they nourish it. When the time is right, up springs new life. No manipulation, no control; perfect freedom, perfect liberty.

—RICHARD FOSTER
*Prayer: Finding the Head's True Home*

# October 3

*Lead me in Your truth and teach me, for You are the God of my salvation.*

PSALM 25:5

Though change is good, it's rarely easy or pleasant. We're most interested in pursuing the comfortable route. We prefer the road more frequently traveled. Everything within us scrambles to stay on trails already blazed. But God often leads us down unknown paths filled with narrow passages and surprising turns.

*—CHARLES R. SWINDOLL*
*Paul: A Man of Grace and Grit*

# *March 29*

*He leads me in the paths of righteousness for His name's sake.*

PSALM 23:3

What the shepherd does with the flock, our Shepherd will do with us. He will lead us to the high country. When the pasture is bare down here. God Will lead us up there. He will guide us through the gate, out of the flatlands, and up the path of the mountain.

—*MAX LUCADO*
*Traveling Light*

## October 2

*Those who dwell under His shadow shall return; they shall be revived like grain, and grow like a vine.*

HOSEA 14:7

God is in the thick of things in your world. He has not taken up residence in a distant galaxy. He has not removed Himself from history. He has not chosen to seclude Himself on a throne in an incandescent castle.

He has drawn near. He has involved Himself in the car pools, heartbreaks, and funeral homes of our day. He is as near to us on Monday as on Sunday. In the school room as in the sanctuary. At the coffee break as much as the communion table.

—MAX LUCADO
*And the Angels were Silent*

# March 30

*He knows the way I take; when He has tried me, I shall come forth as gold.*

JOB 23:10 NASB

The key phrase in that statement is "when He has tried me." You see, there is no hurry-up process for finding and shaping gold. The process of discovering, processing, purifying, and shaping gold is a lengthy, painstaking process. Affliction is gold in the making for the child of God, and God is the one who determines how long the process takes. He alone is the Refiner.

— *CHARLES R. SWINDOLL*

*Joseph*

## October 1

*All things work together for good to those who love God, to those who are the called according to His purpose.*

ROMANS 8:28

As long as we maintain our dependence on God, He is able to take all the evils that befall us and weave them into His master plan. Our omnipotent God can make even "the wrath of man to praise Him." He can take any sins, any evil, any calamity—no matter where it originated—and make it "work together for good to those who love God."

— CATHERINE MARSHALL
*Moments that Matter*

# March 31

*I am going there to prepare a place for you. After I go and prepare a place for you, I will come back and take you to be with Me.*

JOHN 14:2-3 NCV

Note the promise of Jesus. "I will come back and take you to be with Me." Jesus pledges to take us home. He does not delegate this task. He may send missionaries to teach you, angels to protect you, teachers to guide you, singers to inspire you, and physicians to heal you, but He sends no one to take you. He reserves this job for Himself.

—*MAX LUCADO*
*Traveling Light*

# September 30

*He who has a generous eye will be blessed, for he gives of his bread to the poor.*

PROVERBS 22:9

Remind yourself of God's promises regarding generosity. God promises if you sow bountifully, you will reap bountifully. So give! Give abundantly! Even extravagant giving is honored by God. I've never known anyone who went bad because he or she was too generous. Remind yourself of His promises regarding generosity and start giving!

—*CHARLES R. SWINDOLL*
*Day by Day*

# April 1

*God is love.*

I JOHN 4:8

Never question God's great love, for it is as unchangeable a part of God as is His holiness. No matter how terrible your sins, God loves you. Were it not for the love of God, none of us would ever have a chance in the future life. But God is Love! And His love for us is everlasting!

— BILLY GRAHAM
*Peace with God*

# September 29

*Behold, I make all things new.*
REVELATION 21:5

It may not be all that hard to imagine what life in heaven is like. Remember that the best part of getting to heaven is becoming the sorts of persons we were always meant to be, and in our better moments wanted to be, in the loving company of God and all of His children. Once we think of it this way, we can relax while we wait to see with our own eyes what we can only imagine here.

—LEWIS SMEDES
*Keeping Hope Alive*

# April 2

*He will teach us His ways, and we shall walk in His paths.*

MICAH 4:2

When we ask God to guide us, we have to accept by faith that He is doing so. This means that when He closes a door in our faces, we do well not to try to crash that door.

The promise is that the Shepherd will go ahead of the sheep; His method is to clear the way for us.

—CATHERINE MARSHALL
*Moments that Matter*

# September 28

*The Son of Man has come to seek and to save that which was lost.*

LUKE 19:10

God will do what it takes—whatever it takes—to bring His children home.

He is the shepherd in search of His lamb. His legs are scratched, His feet are sore, and His eyes are burning. He scales the cliffs and traverses the fields. He explores the caves. He cups His hands to His mouth and calls into the canyon. And the name He calls is yours.

— MAX LUCADO
*And the Angels were Silent*

*Good and upright is the Lord; therefore He teaches sinners in the way.*

PSALM 25:8

Shame is a deep, dark wound that scars our hearts. When we feel shame, we are vulnerable to attacks and then to deeper shame.

Rather than get caught in shame's downward spiral, we can stop the process by lifting our damaged hearts up to the Lord. We can look to Him for release from the past hurts and relief from the present troubles. Look to the One you can trust for mercy and acceptance.

—PETER WALLACE
*What the Psalmist Is Saying to You*

# September 27

*You, O Lord, are our Father; our Redeemer from Everlasting is Your name.*

ISAIAH 63:16

Nothing can take the place of a daily devotional life with Christ. The great missionary Hudson Taylor said, "Never mind how great the pressure is—only where the pressure lies. Never let it come between you and the Lord, then the *greater* pressure, the more it *presses you* to His heart!" Our quiet time, our prayer time, the time we spend in the Word is absolutely essential for a happy Christian life.

—BILLY GRAHAM
*The Secret of Happiness*

# April 4

*If you have faith as a mustard seed, you will say to this mountain " move from here to there," and it will move.*

MATTHEW 17:20

Don't measure the size of the mountain; talk to the One who can move it. Instead of carrying the world on your shoulders, talk to the One who holds the universe on His. Hope is a look away.

—MAX LUCADO
*Traveling Light*

# September 26

*Men have not heard nor perceived by the ear, nor has the eye seen any God besides You, who acts for the one who waits for Him.*

ISAIAH 64:4

When you wait on the Lord for an answer, you are saying, in effect, "God, I'm here. I reverence You. I fear You with an awesome respect. I love You. And I'm waiting here in Your presence until I hear what You want me to do."

—*LARRY LEA*
*Wisdom: The Gift Worth Seeking*

## *April 5*

*Jesus Christ came into the world to save sinners.*
I TIMOTHY 1:15

God designed and created you because He loves you…. But you drifted in the currents of sin and were swept from Him into the world. He worked for years, making the necessary arrangements to buy you back. Finally everything was ready. The purchase price He counted out was not nickels and dimes and quarters, it was the blood of His own dear Son. As He strode victoriously out of the tomb on Easter morning, you could almost feel Him hugging you to Himself, whispering triumphantly, "You're twice mine! I made you at Creation; now I've bought you at Calvary!"

— ANNE GRAHAM LOTZ
*God's Story*

# *September 25*

*Christ also suffered for us, leaving us an example,
that you should follow His steps.*

I PETER 2:21

Jesus died…on purpose. No surprise. No hesitation. No faltering…. The way Jesus marched to His death leaves no doubt: He had come to earth for this moment.

The journey to the cross didn't begin in Jericho. It didn't begin in Galilee. It didn't begin in Nazareth. It didn't even begin in Bethlehem. The journey to the cross began long before. As the echo of the crunching of the fruit was still sounding in the garden, Jesus was leaving for Calvary.

— MAX LUCADO
*And the Angels were Silent*

# April 6

*The Lord longs to be gracious to you, and therefore He
waits on high to have compassion on you.*

ISAIAH 30:18 NASB

Do you long for God? I've got great news! In an even greater way—greater than you could ever imagine—He longs to be gracious to you. He is offering you all the things you hunger for. The table is loaded, and He is smiling, waiting for you to sit down and enjoy the feast He prepared with you in mind. Have a seat—grace is being served.

—*CHARLES R. SWINDOLL*

*Joseph*

# September 24

*The secret of the Lord is with those who fear Him,*
*and He will show them His covenant.*

PSALM 25:14

When we need help, we wish we knew somebody who is wise enough to tell us what to do, reachable when we need him, and even able to help us. God is. Omniscient, omnipresent, omnipotent—everything we need. The issue is confidence in the Shepherd Himself, a confidence so complete that we offer ourselves without any reservation whatsoever and determine to do what He says.

—ELISABETH ELLIOT
*Keep a Quiet Heart*

# April 7

*I love those who love Me, and those who seek Me diligently will find Me.*

PROVERBS 8:17

The love of God is the very life of God. That life, if allowed to grow freely in the good ground of the well-prepared soil of our souls, will flourish.

Such fruit can and does come only from above. It is not something we can counterfeit. The very life of God, epitomized in the love of God, originates only and always with Hint.

— PHILLIP KELLER
*A Gardener Looks at the Fruits of the Spirit*

## September 23

*God's Word vaults across the skies from*
*sunrise to sunset,…warming hearts to faith.*

PSALM 19:6 THE MESSAGE

When God gets into our hoping, we pin our hopes on a Person. More exactly, on a Person and the promises He makes. Not that He will see to it that we get everything we wish for and believe is possible, but that He will give us what He promises. So now our hope moves from a belief that the good we want is possible to a trust that God intends to keep His promise and is competent to do it.

—LEWIS SMEDES
*Keeping Hope Alive*

## April 8

*Walk in love, just as Christ also loved you and gave Himself up for us.*

EPHESIANS 5:2 NASB

God has not designed us to live like hermits in a cave. He has designed us to live in friendship and fellowship and community with others.

That's why the church, the body of Christ, is so very important, for it is there that we are drawn together in love and mutual encouragement.

We're meant to be a part of one another's lives.

—CHARLES R. SWINDOLL

*Elijah*

# September 22

*The fear of the Lord is the beginning of knowledge.*

PROVERBS 1:7

Wisdom comes from God. It is not something inbred into human nature as an innate ability. Wisdom is a gift or a grace that comes from God, and, like all gifts from God, you must choose to receive it. It's available to you. not only permits you to have it but also desires you to have it. You must accept it, however, and in the accepting lies a choice.

—*LARRY LEA*

*Wisdom: The Gift Worth Seeking*

# April 9

*Your word is a lamp to my feet and a light to my path.*

PSALM 119:105

The more we know of God , the greater is our capacity to love Him. The more we love Him, the greater is our capacity to obey Him. Our *new* affection, however, must be made to grow. We are called to love God with our whole hearts. The *new* heart of flesh must be nurtured. It must be fed by the Word of God.

— R. C. SPROUL
*In the Presence of God*

# September 21

*God has chosen the weak things of the world to put
to shame the things which are mighty.*

I CORINTHIANS 1:27

It is the sublime Spirit of the living God who bestows upon us the
capacity to express genuine concern and compassion for others.
His selfless self-giving enables us to treat others with courtesy and
consideration. This quality is much more than a thin veneer of proper
propriety or superficial politeness. Rather, it is the epitome of a laid-down
life, poured out, lived out on behalf of others.

PHILLIP KELLER

*A Gardener Looks at the Fruits of the Spirit*

# April 10

*The fear of the Lord is the beginning of wisdom, and the knowledge of the Holy One is understanding.*

PROVERBS 9:10

It takes God to make the heart right. When I have a wrong attitude, I look at life humanly. When I have a right attitude, I look at life divinely.

—*CHARLES R. SWINDOLL*

*Joseph*

# September 20

*God is at work within you, helping you want to obey*
*Him, and then helping you do what He wants.*

PHILIPPIANS 2:13 TLB

As a result of being saved, what do we do? We obey God with deep reverence and shrink back from all that might displease Him. Practically put, we love our neighbor and refrain from gossip. We refuse to cheat on taxes and spouses and do our best to love people who are tough to love. Do we do this in order to be saved? No. These are the good things that result from being saved.

— MAX LUCADO
*He Chose the Nails*

# April 11

*If we confess our sins, He is faithful and just to forgive us
our sins and to cleanse us from all unrighteousness.*

I JOHN 1:9

According to Jesus, we all need forgiveness. Knowing we are
inadequate before God and other people leads to compassion, but
thinking we are good before God and others makes us self-centered and
difficult to live with. The better we think we are, the less we can love. The
more we see our need, the more we'll turn for help…and the more we'll
help others because were able to see their need.

—PAUL E. MILLER
*Love Walked Among Us*

## September 19

*The heavens will praise Your wonders, O Lord; Your faithfulness also in the assembly of the saints.*

PSALM 89:5

When God works on behalf of His people, the world will know it. All creation will acknowledge it.

And when God works on behalf of His people, His angels will know it, and will praise His faithfulness.

God is working on your behalf. He is providing everything you need right now to live a fulfilled life.

—PETER WALLACE
*What the Psalmist Is Saying to You*

# April 12

*It is He who has made us, and not we ourselves; we are His people and the sheep of His pasture.*

PSALM 100:3

Sheep aren't the only ones who need a healing touch. We also get irritated with each other, butt heads, and then get wounded. Many of our disappointments in life begin as irritations. The large portion of our problems is not lion-sized attacks, but rather the day-to-day swarm of frustrations and mishaps and heartaches.

— *MAX LUCADO*
*Traveling Light*

## September 18

*Be merciful, just as your Father also is merciful.*

LUKE 6:36

To be kind toward others is merely doing to them what we would like them to do to us. This kindness is linked to mercy. God's love is manifested by and through His mercy. Mercy is an act of kindness. It is also an expression of tenderness.

— R. C. SPROUL

*Loved By God*

# April 13

*Those who know Your name will put their trust in You; for You, Lord, have not forsaken those who seek You.*

PSALM 9:10

The tragedies most difficult to take are those that come through the failures, ignorance, carelessness, or hatred of other human beings. There are times when men seem to be working havoc with God's plans.

But God is adequate even for these situations. In order to fly, the bird must have two wings. One wing is the realization of our human helplessness, the other is the realization of God's power.

— CATHERINE MARSHALL
*Moments that Matter*

## September 17

*This is the day the Lord has made; we will rejoice and be glad in it.*

PSALM 118:24

As we open our eyes each morning, God sets before us a priceless present. Unique, fresh, and full of potential, each day God gives us *time*.

"Rejoice!" the psalmist says. Has God granted you another day? "Rejoice and be glad in it!"…

With each new day, God gives us time as a gracious gift. Rejoice!

—*ALICIA BRITT CHOLE*

*Pure Joy*

# April 14

*When He comes we will be like Him, for we will see Him as He really is.*

I JOHN 3:2 NLT

When the disciples saw Jesus on the Mount of Transfiguration, they got a peek at His glory. He was radiant, beautiful, magnificent. He was Jesus, the Jesus they knew and loved—only *more so*. And we shall be glorious as well. Jesus called Himself the Son of Man to state clearly that He is what mankind was meant to be. What we see in Jesus is our personal destiny.

—JOHN ELDREDGE
*The Journey of Desire*

## September 16

*Blessed are the poor in spirit, for theirs is the kingdom of heaven.*
MATTHEW 5:3

Happy are the meek. Happy are the yielded. Happy are those who trustingly put their lives, their fortunes, and their futures in the capable hands of their Creator. Happy are those who "let go and let God."

—BILLY GRAHAM
*The Secret of Happiness*

*April 15*

*The children of men put their trust under the shadow of Your wings.*

PSALM 36:7

When placed in the light of our awesome God, our lives find new perspective:

Anxiety is replaced by hope when we see that nothing could ever be bigger than God.

Fear loses its strength when we recognize that God's power and love are a million times greater than our weakness and failure.

Peace floods our lives when we remember that all our needs are safely encompassed by God's brilliant sufficiency.

—ALICIA BRITT CHOLE

*Pure Joy*

# *September 15*

*God put the wrong on Him who never did anything
wrong, so we could be put right with God.*

II CORINTHIANS 5:21 THE MESSAGE

The blood of Christ does not cover your sins, conceal your sins, postpone your sins, or diminish your sins. It takes away your sins, once and for all time. Jesus allows your mistakes to be lost in His perfection.

—MAX LUCADO

*He Chose the Nails*

## April 16

*Through love serve one another.*
GALATIANS 5:13

The world urges us to "get, get, get." Christ comes along and says, "Give, give, give." The world says happiness lies in everything from sex to spaghetti. Christ comes along and says our serenity is in knowing Him. The world says make a big splash and show your success by your possessions—impress people. Christ comes along and says the greatest among us is the one who is willing to be a servant.

—PHILLIP KELLER
*A Gardener Looks at the Fruits of the Spirit*

# September 14

*I am like a green olive tree in the house of God; I trust in the mercy of God forever and ever.*

PSALM 52:8

A tree stands in the courtyard. Immovable. Unshakable. With roots deep in the rich earth, drawing strength, support, and sustenance.

An olive tree is evergreen. Always alive, always growing, limbs spreading and greenery flourishing. That was how David pictured himself as a child of God. The question of his place in the world had been settled. He would trust in God's love forever and ever.

— PETER WALLACE
*What the Psalmist Is Saying to You*

# April 17

*He shall stand and feed His flock in the strength of the Lord.*

MICAH 5:4

I have often thought of Jesus' words when He was only hours removed from the cross. In His prayer to the Father,…He said, "I glorified Thee on the earth, having accomplished the work which Thou hast given Me to do" (John 17:4). A little over thirty-three years after His arrival in Bethlehem, there He stood in Jerusalem, saying, in effect, "It's a wrap." He had done everything the Father sent Him to do…and in the final analysis, that's what mattered.

—*CHARLES R. SWINDOLL*
*Day by Day*

# September 13

*Create in me a clean heart, O God, and renew a steadfast spirit within me.*

PSALM 51:10

The late Leonard Bernstein, composer and famed conductor; was asked what he believed to be the most difficult instrument in the orchestra to play. He responded, "Second fiddle!"

When you examine the life of any great individual, you soon discover an entire section of second-fiddlers, super people, gifted in their own rights, but content to play their parts seated in the second chair.

*— CHARLES R. SWINDOLL*
*Paul: A Man of Grace and Grit*

# April 18

*If any of you is having troubles, he should pray.*

JAMES 5:13 NCV

Have you taken your disappointments to God? You've shared them with your neighbor, your relatives, your friends. But have you taken them to God? Before you go anywhere else with your disappointments, go to God.

—MAX LUCADO
*Traveling Light*

# September 12

*Does not the potter have power over the clay?*
ROMANS 9:21

Jesus makes suffering understandable: as the Potter, He uses suffering as the pressure on the wet "clay" of our lives. Under His gentle, loving touch, our lives are molded into a "shape" that pleases Him. But the shape that is so skillfully wrought is not enough. He not only desires our lives to be useful, He also wants our character to be radiant. And so He places us in the furnace of affliction until our "colors" are revealed—colors that reflect the beauty of His own character.

—ANNE GRAHAM LOTZ
*Just Give Me Jesus*

# April 19

*Seek first the kingdom of God and His righteousness,*
*and all these things shall be added to you.*

MATTHEW 6:33

When you live to please God and to keep the inner person healthy, you discover that life gradually becomes *unified*. Instead of running here and there, trying to do everything and please everybody, you calmly face the challenges of each day without feeling pulled apart. You find it's much easier to make decisions because life is centered on one thing: seeking first "the kingdom of God and His righteousness."

—WARREN W. WIERSEBE
*The Twenty Essential Qualities*

# *September 11*

*The Lord does not see as man sees; for man looks at the*
*outward appearance, but the Lord looks at the heart.*

I SAMUEL 16:7

How wonderful that God calls the seemingly unqualified to serve Him. Few of us are the eldest, the brightest, the most beautiful, or the most gifted. But God does not judge us by our outward appearance....

God is not distracted by style, personality, appearance, or achievement. His gaze pierces the flesh and weighs the heart. Then He places His hand upon sincere souls and turns shepherds into kings.

—ALICIA BRITT CHOLE

*Pure Joy*

# April 20

*I have come down from heaven, not to do My own*
*will, but the will of Him who sent Me.*

JOHN 6:38

I'm a list person. Are you? I make my daily list, my weekly list, and my monthly list. I just *love* lists.

Jesus also was a list maker. His list only had one thing on it: to do the will of His Father. You never see Him check things off His list because His list was His lifestyle. His whole life was a ministry of interruptions on His way to the cross.

—ESTHER BURROUGHS
*Splash the Living Water*

# September 10

*I can do all things through Christ who strengthens me.*

PHILIPPIANS 4:13

The suffering you endure can ultimately turn to your benefit. God is working. Only He knows the end from the beginning, and He knows you and your needs far better than even you do. Don't ask "Why is this happening to me?" Rather, ask the question, "How should I respond?" Otherwise, you'll miss the beneficial role suffering plays in life.

—CHARLES R. SWINDOLL

*Paul: A Man of Grace and Grit*

# April 21

*What does the Lord require of you but to do justly, to love
mercy, and to walk humbly with your God?*

MICAH 6:8

L ists are everywhere. The publishing world has its best-seller list, the
music world its gold and platinum album lists, the financial world its
Fortune 500 list.

The prophet Micah lists the absolute basics "required" by the Lord. It's not
a long list. In fact it's short and simple. So the next time you feel that living
for God is getting too complicated, blow the dust off Micah's list: to do
justice, to love kindness, to walk humbly with God.

— *CHARLES R. SWINDOLL*
*Day by Day*

# September 9

*Blessed is the man who…delight[s] in the law of the LORD….*
*He shall be like a tree planted by the rivers of water.*

PSALM 1:1-3

I f you will be faithful in meditating on the Word of God every day…you
will have a wellspring of joy in your life that bubbles up like an artesian
well. It will be like rivers of living water. You won't have to run to and fro
seeking to prime the pump of your spiritual life. The life will be within
you and flowing from you.

—LARRY LEA
*Wisdom: The Gift Worth Seeking*

## April 22

*He will again have compassion on us, and will subdue our iniquities.*
*You will cast all our sins into the depths of the sea.*

MICAH 7:19

A Christian *can* sin, but a Christian does not *have* to sin.

That's an important distinction for you to understand. You *may* commit sin and fall into error. But that's not an automatic certainty. You can develop a new heart to the point that you do *not* sin…. When you accept the Lord Jesus into your life,

God puts a new will within your will. He puts a new spirit inside your spirit.

—LARRY LEA
*Wisdom: The Gift Worth Seeking*

## September 8

*If we live, we live for the Lord; and if we die, we die for the Lord.*
*Whether therefore we live or die, we belong to the Lord.*

ROMANS 14:7-9 NEB

The life and death of all of us is in the same Hands. We are always surrounded by the Unseen, among whom are the angels, ministers of fire, explicitly commissioned to guard us. He who keeps us neither slumbers nor sleeps. His love is always awake, always aware, always surrounding and upholding and protecting. If a spear or a bullet finds its target in the flesh of one of His servants, it is not because of inattention on His part. It is because of love.

—ELISABETH ELLIOT
*The Path of Loneliness*

## April 23

*Give all your worries to Him, because He cares for you.*
I PETER 5:7 NCV

Maybe you don't want to trouble God with your hurts. *After all, He's got famines and pestilence and wars; He won't care about my little struggles,* you think. Why don't you let Him decide that? He cared enough about a wedding to provide the wine. He cared enough about Peter's tax payment to give him a coin. He cared enough about the woman at the well to give her answers.

—MAX LUCADO
*Traveling Light*

# September 7

*God demonstrates His own love toward us, in that while*
*we were still sinners, Christ died for us.*

ROMANS 5:8

The Incarnation, the life and the death of Jesus, answers once and for all the question, "What is God's heart toward me?" That is why Paul says in Romans 5, "Look here, at the Cross. Here is the demonstration of God's heart. At the point of our deepest betrayal, when we had run our farthest from him and gotten so lost in the woods we could never find our way home, God came and died to rescue us."

—BRENT CURTIS AND JOHN ELDREDGE
*The Sacred Romance*

# April 24

*You, Lord, are good and ready to forgive, and abundant
in mercy to all those who call upon You.*

PSALM 86:5

Once we know that nothing we have ever done can get God to reject us because of what we are, we feel free to forgive ourselves for whatever we have *done.* And each time we forgive ourselves we pull our feet out of yesterday's failure and begin to hope again for tomorrow's blessings.

—LEWIS SMEDES
*Keeping Hope Alive*

*Whatever things you ask when you pray, believe that
you receive them, and you will have them.*

MARK 11:24

With God, there is only the infinite NOW. Therefore, by faith we must grasp the fact that all the blessings we shall ever need are already deposited in the Treasury of Heaven.

Money in any checking account will stay right there until the owner cashes a check *in the present.* Even so, we shall receive God's blessings only as we claim them one by one *in the present.* Faith in the future tense is hope—not faith. A sure sign that our hope has passed into faith is when we stop begging God and begin thanking Him for the answer to our prayer.

—*CATHERINE MARSHALL*
*Moments that Matter*

# April 25

*I acknowledged my sin to You, and my iniquity I have not hidden.*

PSALM 32:5

When we repent, God promises restitution and forgiveness through the blood of Jesus Christ. He does not promise relief from any and all consequences, but He promises a relief that only the Spirit of God can give.

—*CHARLES R. SWINDOLL*
*Day by Day*

## September 5

*Having been justified by faith, we have peace
with God through our Lord Jesus Christ.*

ROMANS 5:1

A part from God there is no lasting quenching of our spiritual
hunger and thirst.

Each of us was created in the image and likeness of God. We were made
for God's fellowship, and our hearts can never be satisfied without His
communion. Just as iron is attracted to a magnet, the soul in its state of
hunger is drawn to God.

— *BILLY GRAHAM*
*The Secret of Happiness*

## April 26

*I am the good shepherd. The good shepherd gives His life for the sheep.*
JOHN 10:11

Real meaning to your life is found in the glorious dawn of God's story, which breaks into full revelation in the Person of Jesus Christ.

Because He emptied Himself of all but love, *you can be filled.*

Because His body was broke, *your life can be whole.*

Because His blood was shed, *your sin can be forgiven.*

Because He finished His Father's work, *your life has worth.*

—ANNE GRAHAM LOTZ
*God's Story*

## September 4

*May the God of peace Himself sanctify you completely; and may your whole spirit, soul, and body be preserved blameless.*

I THESSALONIANS 5:23

If we always feel good and look good and lead a good life; if our kids always behave and our home is always orderly and our bank account is always sufficient and we are patient and kind and thoughtful, others shrug because they're capable of that, too.

On the other hand, if we have a splitting headache, the kids are screaming, the phone is ringing, the supper is burning yet we are still patient, kind, and thoughtful, the world sits up and takes notice. The world knows that kind of behavior is not natural. It's supernatural.

—ANNE GRAHAM LOTZ
*Just Give Me Jesus*

## April 27

*When you pass through the waters, I will be with you; and through the rivers, they shall not overflow you.*

ISAIAH 43:2

God does not whisk us at once to Glory. We go on living in a fractured world, suffering in one way or another the effects of sin—sometimes our own, sometimes others'. Yet I have come to understand even suffering, through the transforming power of the Cross, as a gift, for in this broken world, *in* our sorrow, He gives us Himself. *In* our loneliness He comes to meet us.

— ELISABETH ELLIOT
*The Path of Loneliness*

# September 3

*He who believes in Me has everlasting life. I am the bread of life.*

JOHN 6:47-48

When the disciples went into the village, they only brought back food. When the Samaritan woman went into the village, she brought back the entire village. The disciples, who knew the Bread of Life, went for physical bread. The woman, who had just met the Bread of Life, brought the hungry to the Bread of Life whom she knew as the living water. One Messiah. One Samaritan. One village—forever changed.

—ESTHER BURROUGHS
*Splash the Living Water*

## April 28

*The sacrifices of God are a broken spirit, a broken and a contrite heart—these, O God, You will not despise.*

PSALM 51:17

Jesus told the parable of the Prodigal Son to dramatize what He meant by the word *repent*. When the Prodigal Son repented he didn't just sit still and feel sorry about all his sins. He wasn't passive and limp about it. He didn't stay where he was, surrounded by the swine. He got up and left! He turned his feet in the other direction. He sought out his father and humbled himself before him, and then he was forgiven.

—BILLY GRAHAM
*Peace with God*

# September 2

*I press toward the goal for the prize of the upward call of God in Christ Jesus.*

PHILIPPIANS 3:14

God's goal is not to make sure you're happy. No matter how hard it is for you to believe this, it's time to do so. Life is not about your being comfortable and happy and successful and pain free. It is about becoming the man or woman God has called you to be.

Life is not about *you!* It's about God.

— *CHARLES R. SWINDOLL*
*Paul: A Man of Grace and Grit*

*April 29*

*If any of you lacks wisdom, let him ask of God, who gives
to all liberally...and it will be given to him.*

JAMES 1:4

God is not only wise, He is the ground of wisdom. He is not only beautiful, He is the source and standard of all beauty. He is not merely good, He is the norm of all goodness.

He is the source, the ground, the norm, the fountainhead of all love.

— R. C. SPROUL

*Loved By God*

## *September 1*

*God is faithful; He will not let you be tempted beyond what you can bear.*
I CORINTHIANS 10:13 NIV

God came down and lived in this same world as a man. He showed us how to live in this world, subject to its vicissitudes and necessities, that we might be changed—not into an angel or a storybook princess, not wafted into another world, but changed into saints in this world. The secret is *Christ* in *me*, not me in a different set of circumstances.

—ELISABETH ELLIOT
*Keep a Quiet Heart*

## April 30

*The throne of God and of the Lamb shall be in it,*
*and His servants shall serve Him.*

REVELATION 22:3

Many people ask. "Well, what will we do in heaven? Just sit down and enjoy the luxuries of life?" No. The Bible indicates that we will serve God. There will be work to do for God. Our very beings will praise God.

It will be a time of total joy, service, laughter; singing, and praise to God. Imagine serving Him forever and never growing tired!

— BILLY GRAHAM
*Peace with God*

# August 31

*Blessed are all those who put their trust in Him.*

PSALM 2:12

In the race of life, God our heavenly Father has come alongside us through the Person of the Holy Spirit. And when we think we can't go one more step, when our hearts feel heavy, when our minds become dull, when our spirits are burned out, we have the *parakletos*, who comes alongside us, puts His everlasting arms around us, and gently walks with us to the finish.

—ANNE GRAHAM LOTZ

*Just Give Me Jesus*

# May 1

*I will not forget you. See, I have inscribed you on the palms of My hands.*

ISAIAH 49:15-16

Did you think God's silence in your life meant He had forgotten you? Oh, no! God says He has engraved your name on the palms of His hands. He says that a mother could forget her nursing baby at mealtime before He could forget you! You are in God's heart and on His mind every moment. He is fully informed of your circumstances and will bring about change when He knows the time is right.

—ANNE GRAHAM LOTZ
*God's Story*

# August 30

*Every good gift and every perfect gift is from above,*
*and comes down from the Father of lights.*

JAMES 1:17

Rather than racing into the limelight, we need to accept our role in the shadows. Don't promote yourself. Don't push yourself to the front. Let someone else do that. Better yet, let God do that. If you're great, trust me, the word will get out. You'll be found…in God's time. If you're necessary for the plan, God will put you in the right place at just the precise time. God's work is not about us. It's His production, start to finish.

— *CHARLES R. SWINDOLL*
*Paul: A Man of Grace and Grit*

# May 2

*My soul shall be joyful in my God; for He has clothed*
*me with the garments of salvation.*

ISAIAH 61:10

Joy has always been one of the most significant hallmarks of God's people. It is a unique quality of character often confused with happiness.

Joy and happiness are not the same. Each springs from a totally different source.

Happiness comes from the world around me. Joy originates directly with the Spirit of the Living God.

— PHILLIP KELLER
*A Gardener Looks at the Fruits of the Spirit*

# August 29

*Let us, then, feel free to come before Gods throne. Here there is grace.*
*And we can receive mercy and grace to help us when we need it.*

HEBREWS 4:16 NCV

Don't we need someone to trust who is bigger than we are? Aren't we tired of trusting the people of this earth for understanding? Aren't we weary of trusting the things of this earth for strength? A drowning sailor doesn't call on another drowning sailor for help. A pauper knows better than to beg from another pauper. He knows he needs someone who is stronger than he is. Jesus' message is this: I am that person. Trust Me.

— MAX LUCADO
*He Chose the Nails*

# *May 3*

*God will always give [His people] what is right, and*
*He will not be slow to answer them.*

LUKE 18:7 NCV

When we come to God , we make requests; we don't make demands. We come with high hopes and a humble heart. We state what we want, but we pray for what's right. And if God gives us the prison of Rome instead of the mission of Spain, we accept it because we know " *God will always give what is right to His people.*"

We go to Him. We bow before Him, and we *trust in Him*.

— *MAX LUCADO*
*Traveling Light*

# August 28

*You are complete in Him, who is the head of all principality and power.*

COLOSSIANS 2:10

True surrender is not an easy out, calling it quits early in the game. This kind of surrender comes only *after* the night of wrestling. It comes only after we open our hearts to care deeply. Then we choose to surrender, or give over, our deepest desires to God. And with them we give over our hearts, our deepest selves. The freedom and beauty and rest that follow are among the greatest of all surprises.

—*JOHN ELDREDGE*
*The Journey of Desire*

*May 4*

*May [He] establish your hearts blameless in holiness before our God.*

I THESSALONIANS 3:13

No matter how soiled your past, no matter how snarled your present, no matter how hopeless your future seems to be—there's a way out.

There's a sure, safe, everlasting way out—but there's only one! You have only one choice to make.

You can go on being miserable, discontented, frightened and unhappy. Or you can decide now to become the person Jesus promised you could be.

—BILLY GRAHAM
*Peace with God*

# August 27

*The peace of God, which surpasses all understanding, will keep your hearts and minds through Christ Jesus.*

PHILIPPIANS 4:7

The storm was raging. The sea was beating against the rocks in huge, dashing waves. The lightning was flashing, the thunder was roaring, the wind was blowing; but the little bird was asleep in the crevice of the rock, its head serenely under its wing, sound asleep.

In Christ we are relaxed and at peace in the midst of the confusions, bewilderments, and perplexities of this life. The storm rages, but our hearts are at rest.

—BILLY GRAHAM
*Peace with God*

# May 5

*The fruit of the Spirit is in all goodness, righteousness, and truth.*
EPHESIANS 5:9

When Jesus left the earth, He gave us the Comforter, the Counselor, the very presence of God. When the Holy Spirit fills you, it is as if Jesus Himself takes the helm of your life and navigates your course.

When you elect the guidance system called the Holy Spirit, your life moves in the right direction. You are filled with the powerful sense of being deeply loved, since *everything* about Jesus' teaching focuses on love. You know you have enormous worth as a human being.

—NEIL CLARK WARREN
*God Said It, Don't Sweat It*

# August 26

*You were sealed with the Holy Spirit of promise, who
is the guarantee of our inheritance.*

EPHESIANS 1:13-14

Our Holy Spirit is a Person; our Teacher, our Guide, the One who comes along beside us. God is committed to the task of working in us, developing us, and deepening the character traits of His Son in us through the Holy Spirit until we look like Him. We are not on our own in this process. He has given us the person of the Holy Spirit to see that we become like Him in every way.

—ESTHER BURROUGHS
*Splash the Living Water*

# *May 6*

*You are our Father; we are the clay, and You our potter;*
*and all we are the work of Your hand.*

ISAIAH 64:8

God is the Potter, we are the clay. He is the one who gives the commands; we are the ones who obey. He never has to explain Himself; He never has to ask permission. He is shaping us over into the image of His Son, regardless of the pain and heartache that may require. Those lessons are learned a little easier when we remember that we are not in charge, He is.

— CHARLES R. SWINDOLL
*Day by Day*

# August 25

*The Lord is faithful, who will establish you and guard you from the evil one.*

II THESSALONIANS 3:3

Why did Jesus live on earth as long as He did? Why not step into our world just long enough to die for our sins and then leave? Why not a sinless year or week? Why did He have to live a life? To take on our sins is one thing, but to take on our sunburns, our sore throats? To experience death, yes—but to put up with life? To put up with long roads, long days, and short tempers? Why did He do it?

Because He wants you to trust Him.

—MAX LUCADO
*He Chose the Nails*

# May 7

*In the beginning was the Word, and the Word was with God, and the Word was God. He was in the beginning with God.*

JOHN 1:1-2

Jesus is the living expression of what's on God's mind. But He's more. He's the living expression of what's on God's heart. But He's even more. He's the very heart of the Almighty God of the universe laid bare for all to see!

Do you want to know what's on the mind of God? Then look at Jesus! Do you want to know the will of God? Then look at Jesus! Do you want to know what's in the heart of God? *Then look at Jesus!*

—ANNE GRAHAM LOTZ
*Just Give Me Jesus*

# August 24

*Blessed be…the Father of mercies and God of all comfort,*
*who comforts us in all our tribulation.*

II CORINTHIANS 1:3-4

Sometimes we just don't feel like singing or smiling. Matter of fact, there are times it's hypocritical to paste a smile on your face.

It is in those times that I am most thankful for the Scriptures. In God's Word we not only discover His will for our lives, we find words of genuine comfort for those times when life comes unglued.

—*CHARLES R. SWINDOLL*
*Paul: A Man of Grace and Grit*

# May 8

*He has made His wonderful works to be remembered;*
*the Lord is gracious and full of compassion.*

PSALM 111:4

God always does what's right because…that's all He's able to do. He can only do what's right because in His being He's altogether righteous. Because God is love. He's is loving in nature, and all of His actions reflect that love.

— R. C. SPROUL
*Loved By God*

# August 23

*I said, " I will confess my transgressions to the Lord,"*
*and You forgave the iniquity of my sin.*

PSALM 32:5

With God, honesty is without a doubt the best policy. Because He knows everything already. When you commit a sin, acknowledge it to the Lord. Don't try to hide it or stuff it or pretend it didn't happen. It's all out in the brightness of heaven's holy light, whether you see it or not.

When you do, the psalmist assures you of God's forgiveness.

—PETER WALLACE
*What the Psalmist Is Saying to You*

# May 9

*If we are faithless, He remains faithful; He cannot deny Himself.*

II TIMOTHY 2:13

Our moods may shift, but God's doesn't.

Our minds may change, but God's doesn't. Our devotion may falter, but God's never does. Even if we are faithless, He is faithful, for He cannot betray himself. He is a sure God.

—MAX LUCADO
*Traveling Light*

# August 22

*In everything give thanks; for this is the will of God. in Christ Jesus for you.*

I THESSALONIANS 5:18

How can I deal with resentments that smolder inside me? The verse above holds the answer. I am to praise God for *all* things, regardless of where they seem to originate. Doing this, He points out, is the key to receiving the blessings of God. Praise will wash away my resentments.

—CATHERINE MARSHALL

*Moments that Matter*

## May 10

*By faith we understand that the worlds were framed by the word of God,*
*so that the things which are seen were not made of things which are visible.*

HEBREWS 11:3

Faith motivates us to do the will of God. Note the verbs in Hebrews 11: Abel offered an acceptable sacrifice; Noah prepared an ark; Abraham went out; Abraham offered his son; Moses chose Israel over Egypt; and so on. True faith isn't feeling good about what God says; it's *doing* what God says. Faith isn't discussing the will of God; it's obeying the will of God.

—WARREN W. WIERSEBE
*The Twenty Essential Qualities*

*If we are faithless, He remains faithful.*

II TIMOTHY 2:13

There is an old saying among orchardists that "The most heavily laden branches always bow the lowest on the tree."

So it is the generosity of our God that humbles our haughty hearts. It is the depth of Christ's compassion that crumbles the tough crust around our self-centered characters. His own gentle, gracious Spirit displaces our arrogance and self-preoccupation. It leaves us laden with His fruits of lowliness and gentleness.

—PHILLIP KELLER

*A Gardener Looks at the Fruits of the Spirit*

# May 11

*It is God…who has shown in our hearts to give the light of the knowledge of the glory of God.*

II CORINTHIANS 4:6

We do not understand many mysteries, but we accept by faith the fact that at the moment we repent of sin and turn by faith to Jesus Christ we are born again.

It is the infusion of divine life into the human soul,…whereby we become the children of God. We receive the breath of God. Christ through the Holy Spirit takes up residence in our hearts. We are attached to God for eternity.

—BILLY GRAHAM
*Peace with God*

# August 20

*There is one God and one mediator between*
*God and men, the man Christ Jesus.*

1 TIMOTHY 2:5 NIV

Somewhere, sometime, somehow you got tangled up in garbage, and you've been avoiding God. You've allowed a veil of guilt to come between you and your Father. You wonder if you could ever feel close to God again.

God welcomes you. God is not avoiding you. God is not resisting you. The door is open, and God invites you in.

—MAX LUCADO
*He Chose the Nails*

## May 12

*God is love, and he who abides in love abides in God, and God in him.*

I JOHN 4:16

Rigid love is not true love. It is veiled manipulation, a conditional time bomb that explodes when frustrated. Genuine love willingly waits! It isn't pushy or demanding. While it has its limits, its boundaries are far-reaching. It neither clutches nor clings. Real love is not shortsighted, selfish, or insensitive. It detects needs and does what is best for the other person without being told.

—*CHARLES R. SWINDOLL*

*Day by Day*

# August 19

*The testing of your faith produces patience.*

JAMES 1:3

It occurs to me that I've never met anyone young and patient. (To be honest, I've not met many old and patient folks either). We're all in a hurry. We don't like to miss one panel of a revolving door. Patience comes hard in a hurry-up society. Yet, it's an essential quality, cultivated only in extended periods of waiting.

—*CHARLES R. SWINDOLL*

*Paul: A Man of Grace and Grit*

## May 13

*The Lord God will cause righteousness and praise*
*to spring forth before all the nations.*

ISAIAH 61:11

Joy is one of the grand attributes of God Himself. It is an integral part of His character. Joy runs like a sparkling stream of great good will through His makeup. Known as the God of all joy, He rejoices in all His own accomplishments. He is joyful in His own delectable character.

When we discover for ourselves that God our Father really is like this it endears Him to us in a delightful way.

—PHILLIP KELLER
*A Gardener Looks at the Fruits of the Spirit*

## August 18

*If we live in the Spirit, let us also walk in the Spirit.*

GALATIANS 5:25

The Holy Spirit is powerfully at work in your life, hovering over your heart, preparing you to love God. He hovers over your mind, preparing you to understand spiritual things and the truth of His Word. He hovers over your will, preparing you to make decisions that are pleasing to Him. All the powers of God—the same power that hung the stars in place and put the planets in their courses and transformed Earth— now resides in you to energize and strengthen you to become the person God created you to be.

—ANNE GRAHAM LOTZ
*Just Give Me Jesus*

# May 14

*Cast your burden on the Lord, and He shall sustain you;*
*He shall never permit the righteous to be moved.*

PSALM 55:22

From the world's perspective, there are many places you can go to find comfort. But there is only one place you will find a hand to catch your tears and a heart to listen to your every longing. True peace comes only from God. Nothing is so great that God is not greater still.

Is urgency in your heart? Something that threatens your emotional well-being as well as your ability to perform in life? Take it to Jesus.

*— CHARLES STANLEY*
*Into His Presence*

## August 17

*The counsel of the Lord stands forever; the plans of His heart to all generations.*

PSALM 33:11

Note the phrase "the plans of His heart." It takes care of any nightmares you may have about merciless masters, heartless robots, and faceless machines. Since the will of God comes from the heart of God, then His will is the expression of His love.

—WARREN W. WIERSEBE
*The Twenty Essential Qualities*

## May 15

*I sought the Lord, and He heard me, and delivered me from all my fears.*

PSALM 34:4

God created mankind for intimacy with Himself, as His beloved. We see it right at the start, when He gives us the highest freedom of all—the freedom to reject Him. The reason is obvious: love is possible only when it is freely chosen. True love is never constrained; our hearts cannot be taken by force.

—*JOHN ELDREDGE*
*The Journey of Desire*

# August 16

*If by one man's offense many died, much more the grace of God and the
gift by the grace of the one Man, Jesus Christ, abounded to many.*

ROMANS 5:15

We do not come to know God through works—we come to know Him by faith through grace. We cannot work our way toward happiness and heaven; we cannot moralize our way, we cannot reform our way, we cannot buy our way. Salvation comes as a gift of God through Christ.

—BILLY GRAHAM
*The Secret of Happiness*

# May 16

*Call to Me, and I will answer you, and show you great
and mighty things, which you do not know.*

JEREMIAH 33:3

Swings give a feeling of weightlessness—for a few moments you bypass the laws of gravity. For a few moments you fly!

Dreams do much the same thing. Dreams crash the confines of what is and what has been. As our minds dare to see the unseen, our imagination fuels our faith and we begin to trust God for something more.

Some folks are afraid to dream. But connected to God, it is safe to dream. There is freedom to let faith take wings.

—ALICIA BRITT CHOLE

*Pure Joy*

# August 15

*All of you who were baptized into Christ have clothed yourselves with Christ.*
GALATIANS 3:27 NIV

While on the cross, Jesus felt the indignity and disgrace of a criminal. No, He was not guilty. No, He had not committed a sin. And, no, He did not deserve to be sentenced. But you and I were, we had, and we did.

Though we come to the cross dressed in sin, we leave the cross dressed in "garments of salvation" (Isa. 61:10 NIV). Indeed, we leave dressed in Christ Himself.

—*MAX LUCADO*
*He Chose the Nails*

# May 17

*Surely goodness and mercy shall follow me all the days of my life; and I will dwell in the house of the Lord forever.*

PSALM 23:6

What a huge statement. Look at the size of it! Goodness and mercy follow the child of God each and every day! Think of the days that lie ahead. What do you see? Days at home with only toddlers? God will be at your side. Days in a dead-end job? He will walk you through. Days of loneliness? He will take your hand. Surely goodness and mercy shall follow me—not some, not most, not nearly all—but all the days of my life.

—MAX LUCADO
*Traveling Light*

## August 14

*You, O Lord, are our Father; Our Redeemer from Everlasting.*

ISAIAH 63:16

If I am willing to be still in my Master's hand, can I not then be still in everything? He's got the whole world *in His hands!* Never mind whether things come from God Himself or from people—everything comes by His ordination or permission. If I mean to be obedient and submissive to the Lord because He is my Lord, I must not forget that whatever He allows to happen becomes, for *me*, His will at that moment.

—ELISABETH ELLIOT
*Keep a Quiet Heart*

## May 18

*Blessed be the God and Father of our Lord Jesus Christ,*
*who...has begotten us again to a living hope.*

1 PETER 1:3

There's a sense of stability in trusting the Lord. That's how we wait silently and with a sense of confidence. When we wait for God to direct our steps, He does! When we trust Him to meet our needs, He will!

—*CHARLES R. SWINDOLL*
*Day by Day*

# August 13

*The...ones who follow the Lamb...were redeemed from among men.*
REVELATION 14:4

We often think of God's will as a thin, barely visible line drawn with chalk that blurs in bad weather. However; the Scriptures speak of our relationship with God as a *way*, not a line. His will is a path paved with great grace.

God does not play hide and seek with those who have committed their lives to Him. Though the specific placement of His children varies greatly, God's will for us allis quite similar. [He] simply says, "follow Me."

—ALICIA BRITT CHOLE
*Pure Joy*

# May 19

*The Lord is my shepherd; I shall not want.*

PSALM 23:1

What is it like to know that no matter how messed up you might be, the good shepherd looks at you with love, surrounds you with His compassion, envelops you in His arms, and cares for the details of your life? Love begins, not with loving, but with being loved. Being loved gives you the freedom and the resources to love. We can only give what we have received.

—PAUL E. MILLER
*Love Walked Among Us*

# August 12

*The Son of God has come and has given us an understanding,*
*that we may know Him who is true.*

I JOHN 5:20

When you're in the middle of a bad day…aim your hard questions at God, not man. Why? Because in life's darkest hours, there are usually no human beings with adequate answers. Counselors may analyze, associates may sympathize, and experienced friends may empathize. But finite minds and feeble flesh can never satisfy us with the Presence we seek for we truly cry for God Himself, not answers.

—JACK HAYFORD
*How to Live Through a Bad Day*

# May 20

*You will seek the Lord your God, and you will find Him if you seek Him with all your heart and with all your soul.*

DEUTERONOMY 4:29

Do you know God?

If Adam knew Him as a beloved Father, if Abraham knew Him as a Friend, if Moses knew Him as a Redeemer, if David knew Him as his Shepherd, if Daniel knew Him as the Lion Tamer, if Mary Magdalene knew Him as the Bondage Breaker, if Martha knew Him as the Promise Keeper, surely you and I can know Him too!

—ANNE GRAHAM LOTZ
*Just Give Me Jesus*

# August 11

*You will guide me with Your counsel, and afterward receive me to glory.*

PSALM 73:24

Very few individuals jump into exceptional work though most would prefer doing just that. As soon as we walk across that stage and receive that diploma, we're ready for the big time.

Our slick resume makes us look like a combination of Joan of Arc, Winston Churchill, and Mother Theresa.

But that's not God's way. He prepares His servants most often through extended periods of waiting, designed to hone skills and break wills, to shape character and give depth. While He works, we wait.

— *CHARLES R. SWINDOLL*
*Paul: A Man of Grace and Grit*

## May 21

*In all these things we are more than conquerors through Him who loved us.*

ROMANS 8:37

Even after generations of people had spit in His face, God still loved them. After a nation of chosen ones had stripped Him naked and ripped His incarnated flesh, He still died for them. And even today, after billions have chosen to prostitute themselves before the pimps of power, fame, and wealth, He still waits for them.

It *is* inexplicable. It doesn't have a drop of logic nor a thread of rationality. And yet, it is that very irrationality that gives the gospel its greatest defense. For only God could love like that.

—*MAX LUCADO*
*God Came Near*

# August 10

*Looking unto Jesus, the author and finisher of our faith....*

HEBREWS 12:2

Jesus is Lord, and this is the primary positive confession that should define our lives. Humility is our bread, obedience our wine. We gain true humility not by putting ourselves down but by standing next to Christ. Once we see how great is the Savior's love for us, we know our lovely place in the world. Humility thus gained is power and triumph.

—*CALVIN MILLER*
*Into the Depths of God*

# May 22

*Though your sins are like scarlet, they shall be as white as snow.*

ISAIAH 1:18

If we were declared 99.9% righteous, some verses would have to be rewritten. Like Isaiah 1:18, which might then read: "Come now, and let us reason together," says the Lord, "though your sins are as scarlet, they will be light pink."

Nonsense! The promise of sins forgiven is all or nothing.

— *CHARLES R. SWINDOLL*

*Day by Day*

# August 9

*I am the good shepherd; and I know My sheep, and am known by My own.*
JOHN 10:14

Jesus looked out at the approaching crowds and saw people who were seeking God. He saw people as more important than His own plans and need for rest.

He saw people not as an interruption, but as an opportunity to reveal His loving care and His Father's compassionate power to meet their deepest needs.

He saw people as sheep who needed a shepherd. He saw people *as God saw them.*

—ANNE GRAHAM LOTZ
*Just Give Me Jesus*

# May 23

*Let the peace of God rule in your hearts.*
COLOSSIANS 3:15

The Greek word "rule" in this verse means "on top of everything else." It's the idea of something being the best.

In the first century this word was used to describe the kind of authority a judge had in a court of law or an umpire today has on an athletic field. Paul meant that the peace of God in our lives should act as a judge or an umpire when it comes to knowing God's will. When we have to make a decision or we're struggling about what to do, we should let the peace of God have a final say.

—*JOHN HULL AND TIM ELMORE*
*Pivotal Praying*

*August 8*

*I will dwell in them and walk among them. I will be their God.*

II CORINTHIANS 6:16

The Christian life is full of paradox (as if you hadn't noticed). Listen to how Paul describes his experience of the quest: "Sorrowful, yet always rejoicing; poor, yet making many rich; having nothing, and yet possessing everything" (II Cor. 6:10, NIV). How true this is. If we will remain open to sorrow, we can know joy. Somehow being empty allows us to make others rich. And if we are willing to let go, we'll discover something most surprising—that all is ours.

—JOHN ELDREDGE
*The Journey of Desire*

# May 24

*Who shall bring a charge against Gods elect? It is God who justifies.*

ROMANS 8:33

Your sins have been forgiven. God has buried them in the depths of the sea and placed them behind His back of forgetfulness. Every sin is completely wiped out. You stood before God as a debtor, you received your discharge, you have become reconciled to God. You are now a child of God.

—BILLY GRAHAM
*Peace with God*

# August 7

*We are made holy through the sacrifice of His body. Christ made this sacrifice only once, and for all time.*

HEBREWS 10:10 NCV

The Son of God became the Lamb of God, the cross became the altar, and we were made holy through the sacrifice Christ made in His body once and for all time.

What needed to be paid was paid. What had to be done was done. Innocent blood was required. Innocent blood was offered, once and for all time. Bury those five words deep in your heart. *Once and for all time.*

—MAX LUCADO
*He Chose the Nails*

# May 25

*We shall not all sleep, but we shall all be changed-in a moment,*
*in the twinkling of an eye, at the last trumpet.*

I CORINTHIANS 15:51-52

When Jesus went home He left the back door open. As a result, "we will all be changed—in a moment, in the twinkling of an eye."

The first moment of transformation went unnoticed by the world. But you can bet your sweet September the second one won't. The next time you use the phrase "just a moment…" remember that's all the time it will take to change this world.

—MAX LUCADO
*God Came Near*

## August 6

*Love your enemies, bless those who curse you, do good to those who hate you.*
MATTHEW 5:44

When Jesus commands us to love our enemies, He defines that love not so much in terms of feelings of affection but in terms of actions. To love our enemies requires that we bless them when they curse us and do good to them when they hate us. This is what it means to mirror and reflect the love of God, because God does good to those who hate Him and blesses people while they are cursing Him.

—R. C. SPROUL
*Loved By God*

# May 26

*All things were made through Him, and without Him nothing was made that was made.*

JOHN 1:3

God created atoms and angels and ants, crocodiles and chiggers and clouds, diamonds and dust and dinosaurs, raindrops and sweat drops, dewdrops and blood drops, and me! And you!

The greatness of His power to create and design and form and mold and make and build and arrange defies the limits of our imagination. And since He created everything, there is nothing beyond His power to fix or mend or heal or restore.

—ANNE GRAHAM LOTZ
*Just Give Me Jesus*

# August 5

*I, the Lord, have called You in righteousness, and will hold Your hand.*

ISAIAH 42:6

A re you filled with anxiety and worry about some problem, wondering what will happen? Listen: As a child of God through faith in Christ, you can turn these over to Christ, knowing that He loves you and is able to help you. At times He may take the problem away; other times He may give you strength to bear it. But you can rest in Him.

—BILLY GRAHAM
*The Secret of Happiness*

# May 27

*The just shall live by faith.*

ROMANS 1:17

Faith actually means surrender and commitment to the claims of Christ. It means an acknowledgment of sin and a turning to Christ. We do not know Christ through the five physical senses, but we know Him through the sixth sense that God has given every person—that ability to believe.

—BILLY GRAHAM
*Peace with God*

# *August 4*

*All things work together for good to those who love God, to those who are the called according to His purpose.*

ROMANS 8:28

God didn't create you to be a failure or a sinner. He created you in Christ Jesus to be righteousness. He created you to live a life that is more abundant.

Your genetic makeup, your family history, or your past experiences don't dictate your future. God holds your future in His hands, and He has promised to work all things together for your GOOD as long as you love and trust Him.

—*LARRY LEA*

*Wisdom: The Gift Worth Seeking*

## May 28

*Oh, taste and see that the Lord is good. Blessed is the man who trusts in Him!*

PSALM 34:8

*T*aste the Lord. It's an unusual invitation. The Hebrew word for *taste* means "to taste or eat, to discern, perceive, evaluate." The idea is of tasting something to see whether it's good to eat for sustenance and strength.

Taste life with God, and see how good it is. It's a life of blessed fulfillment.

—PETER WALLACE
*What the Psalmist Is Saying to You*

# August 3

*God makes His people strong. God gives His people peace.*

PSALM 29:11 THE MESSAGE

When God plans to use us, He puts us through the paces. He allows a certain amount of suffering. God may use the strong, stubborn, independent individualists in the world, but not long-term. He much prefers the humble, the broken, the bruised, the humble, even the crushed. He works much more effectively in the lives of people who've learned they can't make it on their own, especially those who acknowledge they desperately need God and others.

—CHARLES R. SWINDOLL
*Paul: A Man of Grace and Grit*

# May 29

*We love Him because He first loved us.*

I JOHN 4:19

Jesus.... Have you seen Him? Those who first did were never the same.

"My Lord and my God!" cried Thomas.

"I have seen the Lord," exclaimed Mary Magdalene.

"We have seen His glory," declared John.

But Peter said it best. "We were eyewitnesses of His majesty."

All the splendor of heaven revealed in a human body.

— MAX LUCADO
*God Came Near*

*The generous soul will be made rich,
and he who waters will also be watered himself*

PROVERBS 11:25

Whatever we may own, whether in large or small measure, when placed gladly in God's great strong hands can be blessed and multiplied a thousand times to enrich countless other lives. If clutched tightly and timidly to our own selfish souls it will shrivel away to a mere whimsy, wasted on one's self.

—PHILLIP KELLER
*A Gardener Looks at the Fruits of the Spirit*

## May 30

*I will never leave you nor forsake you.*

HEBREWS 13:5

The Love that calls us into being, woos us to Himself, makes us His bride, lays down His life for us, and daily crowns us with loving-kindness and tender mercy, will *not*, no matter how it may appear in our loneliness, abandon us. "I will never [the Greek has five different negatives here], never, never, never, never leave you or forsake you."

—ELISABETH ELLIOT
*The Path of Loneliness*

# August 1

*Those who wait on the Lord shall renew their strength;*
*they shall mount up with wings like eagles.*

ISAIAH 40:31

Waiting is part of ordinary time. We discover God in our waiting: waiting in checkout lines, waiting for the telephone to ring, waiting for graduation, waiting for a promotion, waiting to retire, waiting to die. The waiting itself becomes prayer as we give our waiting to God. In waiting we begin to get in touch with the rhythms of life—stillness and action, listening and decision. They are the rhythms of God. It is in the everyday and the commonplace that we learn patience, acceptance, and contentment.

—*RICHARD FOSTER*
*Prayer: Finding the Heart's True Home*

# May 31

*You are God, ready to pardon, gracious and merciful.*
NEHEMIAH 9:17

Don't get stuck on where you *were*. Don't waste your time focusing on *what you used to be*. Remember, the hope we have in Christ means there's a brighter tomorrow. The sins are forgiven. The shame is canceled out. Were no longer chained to a deep, dark pit of the past. Grace gives us wings to soar beyond it.

— *CHARLES R. SWINDOLL*
*Paul: A Man of Grace and Grit*

# July 31

*I will sing of the mercies of the Lord forever; with my mouth will I make known Your faithfulness to all generations.*

PSALM 89:1

Henri Nouwen once asked Mother Teresa for spiritual direction. "Spend one hour each day in adoration of your Lord," she said, "and never do anything you know is wrong. Follow this, and you'll be fine." Such simple, yet profound advice. Worship is the act of the abandoned heart adoring God.

—JOHN ELDREDGE
*The Journey of Desire*

## June 1

*The Lord also will be a refuge...in times of trouble.*

PSALM 9:9

Refuge. A shelter from danger or trouble.

A place to go for safety.

Run to the outstretched arms of the Lord.

For He will wrap you up in His love, surround you with His power, and protect you.

He is *your* refuge. And He is waiting to welcome you.

—PETER WALLACE
*What the Psalmist Is Saying to You*

# July 30

*Be tenderhearted, be courteous...that you may inherit a blessing.*

I PETER 3:8-9

Inevitably, when we stand strong and alone like a steer in a blizzard, looking like we can make it on our own, we easily forget that each life-sustaining beat of our hearts is a gift from God—we're really not that independent after all.

We not only need the Lord, we need each other. That need only intensifies when the barometer of life drops to the bottom of the gauge—when the winds of adversity blow hard against our souls. We cannot make it on our own.

—*CHARLES R. SWINDOLL*
*Paul: A Man of Grace and Grit*

# June 2

*He will love you and bless you and multiply you.*
DEUTERONOMY 7:13

God is the Good Gardener who toils over us and tends us with constant care. Patiently He waits for the full fruitage. He finds joy in the planting He has done and waits eagerly for a crop. With great joy He gathers the harvest.

There is a deep delight in all He does. There is enthusiasm in everything He undertakes. There is sweet satisfaction in all His enterprises. His life, vitality, and energy are transmitted directly to me by His Spirit who resides within.

—PHILLIP KELLER
*A Gardener Looks at the Fruits of the Spirit*

*July 29*

*I will strengthen you, yes, I will help you. I will*
*uphold you with My righteous right hand.*

ISAIAH 41:10

Whatever the circumstances, whatever the call, whatever the duty, whatever the price, whatever the sacrifice—God's strength will be your strength in your hour of need.

—BILLY GRAHAM
*Peace with God*

# June 3

*His divine power has given to us all things that pertain to life and godliness, through the knowledge of Him who called us by glory and virtue.*

II PETER 1:3

God is bigger than we think and greater than we think. Nothing is beyond His ability, whether it's a problem to solve, a marriage to reconcile, a memory to heal, a guilty conscience to cleanse, or a sin to forgive.

If God has the power to create and sustain the universe, *how can you think His power is insufficient for you?* He is more than able to sustain your marriage and your ministry, your faith and your finances, your hope and your health.

— ANNE GRAHAM LOTZ
*Just Give Me Jesus*

## July 28

*Give us this day our daily bread.*

MATTHEW 6:11

Jesus invites us to pray for daily bread.

In doing so, He has transfigured the trivialities of everyday life. Try to imagine what our prayer experience would be like if He had forbidden us to ask for the little things. What if the only things we were allowed to talk about were the weighty matters, the important things, the profound issues? We would be orphaned in the cosmos, cold, and terribly alone. But the opposite is true; He welcomes us with our 1,001 trifles, for they are each important to Him.

—*RICHARD FOSTER*
*Prayer: Finding the Heart's True Home*

# June 4

*'I will feed My flock, and I will make them lie down;' says the Lord God.*

EZEKIEL 34:15

There is not a hint of one person who was afraid to draw near Jesus. There were those who mocked Him. There were those who were envious of Him. There were those who misunderstood Him. There were those who revered Him. But there was not one person who considered Him too holy, too divine, or too celestial to touch. *There was not one person who was reluctant to approach Him for fear of being rejected.*

—MAX LUCADO

*God Came Near*

# July 27

*The eyes of the Lord run to and fro throughout the whole earth, to show Himself strong on behalf of those whose heart is loyal to Him.*

II CHRONICLES 16:9

In God's kingdom, comparisons are not allowed. We make a terrible mistake comparing. God does not have a standard by which He measures us against each other. We do that. His standard is far higher. Holy God measures each of us against His Son, Jesus. That should change your focus. God will not ask if we wear specific clothing labels, He will want to know if we are clothed in Christ Jesus.

—ESTHER BURROUGHS
*Splash the Living Water*

# June 5

*Neither death nor life, nor angels nor principalities nor powers, nor things present nor things to come, nor height nor depth, nor any other created thing, shall be able to separate us from the love of God.*

ROMANS 8:38-39

In this passage the apostle sets forth the principle that gripped the reformers of the sixteenth century: *Deus pro nobis,* which means simply "God for us." The source of Christian comfort is that God is for us and is on our side. To know that God is for us is to know that no one and nothing can ever prevail against us.

—*R. C. SPROUL*
*Loved By God*

## July 26

*"Surely I am coming quickly."*
*Amen. Even so, come, Lord Jesus.*

REVELATION 22:20

The Lord Jesus is coming back! That's how much He loves us. The plan of salvation is not only to satisfy us in this world and give us a new life here, but He has a great plan for the future. For eternity!

—*BILLY GRAHAM*
*Peace with God*

# *June 6*

*Draw near to God and He will draw near to you.*

JAMES 4:8

Some people find it easier to draw closer to God in magnificent buildings and with some form of ritual. Others find they can seek God only in stark simplicity. Some people find themselves more comfortable with formality, others feel more at home with informality. The important thing is not *how* we do it, but the sincerity and depth of purpose *with which* we do it.

— BILLY GRAHAM
*Peace with God*

## July 25

*We are His workmanship, created in Christ Jesus for good works.*

EPHESIANS 2:10

Although God cares about financial stability, world peace, and social justice, He has one great thing on His mind today—you. You are His workmanship, His masterpiece. There is no one else exactly like you, and God cares for you with infinite watchfulness. He knows exactly how many hairs came out in your brush this morning. Your checkbook matters as much as the federal budget, harmony in your home as much as harmony among nations.

—CHARLES STANLEY
*Into His Presence*

# June 7

*If you forgive men their trespasses, your heavenly Father will also forgive you.*

MATTHEW 6:14

**P**rayerfully letting go of wrongs or injustices caused by others is hard. But if we're to experience God's best for our lives, we have to learn to let go. Letting go and allowing God to work toward healing our wounds will bring peace of mind and clarity of conscience. Letting go means forgiving. Plain and simple. The Greek word for *forgive* means "to let go."

—JOHN HULL AND TIM ELMORE
*Pivotal Praying*

# July 24

*How precious is Your lovingkindness, O God! Therefore the children*
*of men put their trust under the shadow of Your wings.*

PSALM 36:7

The Hebrew word for *lovingkindness* means "unfailing love, steadfast love, mercy, goodness." God extends lovingkindness to us, His children. Like a mother hen brooding over her chicks, the Father invites you under His wings to be protected, warmed, and filled. There, you can relax and rest.

—PETER WALLACE
*What the Psalmist Is Saying to You*

# June 8

*Is anyone among you suffering?*
*Let him pray…and the Lord will raise him up.*

JAMES 5:13-15

Depression is a gloomy mindset that from time to time smudges our moods. At one time or another it afflicts us all. The waves of depression crash upon the shores of our lives in ever-increasing surges.

But is it hopeless? No. Christ is always the key to winning over our dour moods. The issue of our wholeness lies in making Christ the Lord over all circumstances.

—*CALVIN MILLER*
*Into the Depths of God*

# July 23

*Where can I flee from Your presence? If I take the wings of the morning, and dwell in the uttermost parts of the sea, even there Your hand shall lead me.*

PSALM 139:7, 9

Our asking "Where is God?" is like a fish asking "Where is water?" or a bird asking "where is air?" God is everywhere! Equally present in Peking and Peoria. As active in the lives of Icelanders as in the lives of Texans.

We cannot find a place where God is not.

—MAX LUCADO
*He Chose the Nails*

# June 9

*The ways of man are before the eyes of the Lord, and He ponders all his paths.*

PROVERBS 5:21

All Abraham knew was that God wanted him to move. He didn't have a clue about the final destination. Nothing about the weather or the crime rate in the area. No information about the neighborhood he'd live in or the problems he would have to face. Nothing. He knew only that God had told him to go.

If you're waiting on God to fill in all the shading in your picture, you will never take the first step in obeying His will. You must be prepared to trust His plan, *knowing* it will be full of surprises.

— CHARLES R. SWINDOLL
*Paul: A Man of Grace and Grit*

# July 22

*Our light affliction, which is but for a moment, is working for
us a far more exceeding and eternal weight of glory.*

II CORINTHIANS 4:17

Life is now a battle and a journey. This is the truest explanation for what is going on, the only way to rightly understand our experience. Life is not a game of striving and indulgence. It is not a long march of duty and obligation. Life is a desperate quest through dangerous country to a destination that is, beyond all our wildest hopes, indescribably good.

— *JOHN ELDREDGE*
*The Journey of Desire*

# June 10

*When Your words came, I ate them; they were my joy and my heart's delight, for I bear Your name, O Lord God Almighty.*

JEREMIAH 15:16 NIV

For me, good company enriches any meal. And Jeremiah felt the same way. His favorite food was God's Word in the company of...God Himself!

What an incredible banquet God gives us through His Word. The Scriptures, when ingested, bring delight to our hearts and energy to our spirits. God's Word is thoroughly nutritious and always fresh.

—ALICIA BRITT CHOLE
*Pure Joy*

# July 21

*Whatever you do, do it heartily, as to the Lord and not to men, knowing that from the Lord you will receive the reward of the inheritance.*

COLOSSIANS 3:23

You may be one of those individuals desperately seeking a way off the treadmill. My advice to you is to stop trying to be the tops in your field. Be an excellent *whatever*. Do the very best you can with what God has given you. If His plan includes bringing you to higher levels of success, He'll do that, in His time, according to His master plan. Your part is to get out of the traffic and set your mind on kingdom priorities—stuff that *really* matters. God is good.

—CHARLES R. SWINDOLL
*Paul: A Man of Grace and Grit*

# June 11

*Whoever desires to save his life will lose it, but whoever loses his life for My sake will find it.*

MATTHEW 16:25

I believe the secret of happiness lies imbedded in those words, painful though they appear to be. I have observed that when any of us embarks on the pursuit of happiness for ourselves, it eludes us. Often I've asked myself why. It must be because happiness comes to us only as a dividend. When we become absorbed in something demanding and worthwhile above and beyond ourselves, happiness seems to be there as a by-product of self-giving.

— CATHERINE MARSHALL
*Moments that Matter*

## July 20

*Righteousness and justice are the foundation of Your*
*throne; mercy and truth go before Your face.*

PSALM 89:14

Pinning our hopes on promises always boils down in the end to one thing: *trust in the person who makes them.*

Trust the Maker of the universe to keep His promises. It is the ultimate fallback: hope.

—*LEWIS SMEDES*
*Keeping Hope Alive*

# June 12

*The number of God's years is unsearchable.*

JOB 36:26 NCV

We may search out the moment the first wave slapped on a shore or the first star burst in the sky, but we'll never find the first moment when God was God, for there is no moment when God was not God. He has never *not been*, for He is eternal. God is not bound by time.

—MAX LUCADO
*He Chose the Nails*

# July 19

*Well done, good and faithful servant; you were faithful over a few things, I will make you ruler over many things.*

MATTHEW 25:21

The Cross is a sign of loss—shameful, humiliating, abject, total loss. Yet it was Jesus' loss that meant heavenly gain for the whole world. Although secured in a tomb with a heavy stone, a seal, and posted guards, He could not be held down by death. He came out of the grave as the Death of Death and Hell's Destruction.

His death was a new beginning. Those who accept that truth receive not only the promise of heaven, but the possibility of heaven on earth, where the Risen Christ walks with us.

*— ELISABETH ELLIOT*
*The Path of Loneliness*

# June 13

*Show me Your ways, O Lord; teach me Your paths.*
PSALM 25:4

The path of peace which God's Word instructs us to pursue is not strewn with rose petals. It's a tough trail tramped out with a humble heart and lowly spirit.

Peace is the spirit and soul of persons so imbued with the presence of God's Gracious Spirit that they are not easily provoked. It is the quiet, potent, gracious attitude of serenity and good will that meets the angry onslaught of others with good cheer, equanimity, and strong repose.

—PHILLIP KELLER
*A Gardener Looks at the Fruits of the Spirit*

# July 18

*Blessed are those who keep His testimonies, who seek Him with the whole heart!*

PSALM 119:2

Have you ever thought of going to church as a divine appointment? Have you ever thought of Bible study as a divine appointment? That Jesus is patiently, personally waiting to meet with you there?

What a difference it would make in our attitude of expectancy and our habit of consistency if we truly wrapped our hearts around the knowledge that each is a divine appointment; that Jesus Himself is waiting to meet with us.

—ANNE GRAHAM LOTZ
*Just Give Me Jesus*

# June 14

*For this is God, our God forever and ever; He will he our guide even to death.*

PSALM 48:14

We live in a culture that regularly confuses humanity with deity. It's the kind of sloppy theology that suggests God sits on the edge of heaven thinking, *Wonder what they'll do next?* How absurd! God is omniscient. This implies, clearly, God never learns anything, our sinful decision and evil deeds notwithstanding. Nothing ever surprises Him. From the moment we're conceived to the moment we die, we remain safely within the frame of His watchful gaze as well as His sovereign plan.

— *CHARLES R. SWINDOLL*
*Paul: A Man of Grace and Grit*

# July 17

*They shall reign forever and ever.*

REVELATION 22:5

Think for a moment. The One who created you and set all those loves and gifts in your heart, the One who has shaped all your life experiences (including the ones that seem to make no sense), this God has prepared a place for you that is a more than perfect fit for all your gifts and quirks and personality traits—even those you don't know you have. Christ is not joking when He says that we shall inherit the kingdom prepared for us and shall reign with Him forever.

—JOHN ELDREDGE
*The Journey of Desire*

# June 15

*I thank you, High God—you're breathtaking!*
*Body and soul, I am marvelously made!*
PSALM 139:14 THE MESSAGE

God wanted to show the world something of His strength. Is He not a great warrior? Has He not performed the daring rescue of His beloved? And this is why He gave us the sculpture that is man. Men bear the image of God in their dangerous, yet inviting strength. Women, too, bear the image of God, but in a much different way. Is not God a being of great mystery and beauty? Is there not something tender and alluring about the essence of the Divine? And this is why He gave us the sculpture that is woman.

—JOHN ELDREDGE
*The Journey of Desire*

# July 16

*He bruises, but He binds up; He wounds, but His hands make whole.*

JOB 5:18

Oh, the hands of Jesus. Hands of incarnation at His birth. Hands of liberation as He healed. Hands of inspiration as He taught. Hands of dedication as He served. And hands of salvation as He died.

The same hand that stilled the seas stills your guilt.

The same hand that cleansed the Temple cleanses your heart.

The hand is the hand of God.

— MAX LUCADO
*He Chase the Nails*

## June 16

*The joy of the Lord is your strength.*
NEHEMIAH 8:10

One of the characteristics of the Christian is an inward joy that does not depend upon circumstances.

S. D. Gordon, said of joy: "Joy is distinctly a Christian word and a Christian thing. It is the reverse of happiness. Happiness is the result of what happens of an agreeable sort. Joy has its springs deep down inside. And that spring never runs dry, no matter what happens." Only Jesus gives that joy.

—*BILLY GRAHAM*
*Peace with God*

# July 15

*Let a man so consider us as servants of Christ and stewards of the mysteries of God. Moreover it is required in stewards that one be found faithful.*

I CORINTHIANS 4:1-2

Christ is the grand over-comer. By receiving Jesus into our lives, we erect the inner bracing that enables us to withstand the pressure of all our outer circumstances. Welcoming Christ into our lives, we gain the power to control life and not be crushed by it. Yet to withstand the crush of life, we must always be submitted to His inner lordship. The yielded life becomes the strong life.

— CALVIN MILLER
*Into the Depths of God*

## June 17

*For He is our God, and we are the people
of His pasture, and the sheep of His hand.*

PSALM 95:7

When the devil comes to tell you about your past, tell him about his past—that he was cast out of heaven and defeated by the blood of Jesus Christ shed on the cross of Calvary.

When the devil comes to taunt you and to paint a negative picture about your future, tell him about his future—that he will burn in the lake of fire forever and that he will never be allowed back into heaven, where you will be spending all of eternity.

—*LARRY LEA*
*Wisdom: The Gift Worth Seeking*

# July 14

*The Helper; the Holy Spirit, whom the Father will send in My name,*
*He will teach you all things, and bring to your*
*remembrance all things that I said to you.*

JOHN 14:26

Today, many agree on what is absolutely evil and absolutely good. But in a world of ever-expanding shades of gray, we can lose confidence in our ability to distinguish where light ends and darkness begins.

Yet God always sees clearly. When faced with a specific decision, let us first look to His Word and ask a simple question: *Can I picture God smiling over this choice?*

God's Spirit will be faithful to teach us and guide us into all truth.

—ALICIA BRITT CHOLE
*Pure Joy*

# June 18

*Of His fullness we have all received, and grace for grace.*

JOHN 1:16

As children of God, we are the primary recipients of His blessing.

When the Mediterranean Sea evaporates or runs low, the Atlantic Ocean rushes in at the Strait of Gibraltar to replenish it and keep it full. When you and I are related to Jesus Christ, our strength and wisdom and peace and joy and hope may run out, but His life rushes in to keep us filled to the brim.

—ANNE GRAHAM LOTZ
*Just Give Me Jesus*

# July 13

*Who is the man that fears the Lord? Him shall He teach in the way He chooses.*

PSALM 25:12

"It's not fair," we say. It's not fair that I was born in poverty or that I sing so poorly or that I run so slowly. But the scales of life were forever tipped on the side of fairness when God planted a tree in the Garden of Eden. All complaints were silenced when Adam and his descendants were given free will, the freedom to make whatever eternal choice we desire. Any injustice in this life is offset by the honor of choosing our destiny in the next.

—MAX LUCADO
*He Chose the Nails*

# June 19

*God is not the author of confusion but of peace.*

I CORINTHIANS 14:33

A t times God's plan will frighten you. Or you'll be intimidated by its demands. Other times you'll be disappointed. For instance, when God tells you no, to wait, or to sit tight, you'll want to argue. You may decide to fight. You might attempt to negotiate. You may become angry. But when your faith kicks in gear, none of those impulses will control you. Faith says, "I can do this. I trust You, Lord. I don't understand everything, but I trust You completely."

*— CHARLES R. SWINDOLL*
*Paul: A Man of Grace and Grit*

# July 12

*Having been justified by faith, we have peace with God.*
ROMANS 5:1

Many of us have entered the Christian life by faith. But having entered, we are inclined to shift our ground. We come to feel that we will become righteous (that is, remain acceptable to God) only as we do certain things.

Yet with a concerted voice, the New Testament writers teach that God's supreme interest is in what we *are*, not what we do.

— *CATHERINE MARSHALL*
*Moments that Matter*

## June 20

*His compassions fail not. They are new every morning;*
*great is Your faithfulness.*
LAMENTATIONS 3:22-23

Some of us know very little of suffering, but we know disappointments and betrayals and losses and bitterness. Are we really meant to thank God for such things? Let's be clear about one thing. God does not cause all the things we don't like. But He does permit them to happen because it is in this fallen world that we humans must learn to walk by faith. He doesn't leave us to ourselves, however. He shares every step.

—ELISABETH ELLIOT
*Keep a Quiet Heart*

# July 11

*Not a word failed of any good thing which the Lord had
spoken to the house of Israel. All came to pass.*

JOSHUA 21:45

The Word of God and the Word of God alone is the basis for our faith.
It reveals the character of God and records His mighty works, both of
which encourage us to believe and obey. The precepts of God reveal His
will, and we can obey them by faith because God's commandments are
still God's enablements. The promises of God are dependable.

—*WARREN W. WIERSEBE*
*The Twenty Essential Qualities*

## *June 21*

*Be of good comfort, be of one mind, live in peace; and
the God of love and peace will be with you.*

II CORINTHIANS 13:11

Marriage is a holy bond because it permits two people to help each other work out their spiritual destinies. God declared marriage to be good because He knew that man needed a helpmate and woman needed a protector. He desires that husbands and wives never lose sight of the original purpose of marriage. It is woman's role to love and help and reassure her husband in every way she can, and it is man's role to love and protect and provide for his wife and the children she bears, so that the home may be filled with God's peace and harmony.

— BILLY GRAHAM
*Peace with God*

## July 10

*Great is our Lord, and mighty in power; His understanding is infinite.*

PSALM 147:5

No means of measure can define God's limitless love. No barrier can hinder Him from pouring out His blessings.

He forgives and He forgets. He creates and He cleanses.

He restores and He rebuilds. He comforts and He carries.

He lifts and He loves. He is the God of the second chance.

—ANNE GRAHAM LOTZ
*Just Give Me Jesus*

# June 22

*Your Redeemer is the Holy One of Israel;*
*He is called the God of the whole earth.*

ISAIAH 54:5

We wonder with so many miraculous testimonies around us, how we could escape God. But somehow we do. We live in an art gallery of divine creativity and yet are content to gaze only at the carpet.

The next time you hear a baby laugh or see an ocean wave, take note. Pause and listen as His Majesty whispers ever so gently, "I'm here."

—MAX LUCADO
*God Came Near*

## July 9

*It is God who works in you both to will and to do for His good pleasure.*

PHILIPPIANS 2:13

For the child of God the development of patience has two enormous benefits. First it produces within our character tremendous strength and endurance. Secondly, as we are patient under adversity we discover the great faithfulness of our God in every situation.

— PHILLIP KELLER

*A Gardener Looks at the Fruits of the Spirit*

## June 23

*You know me inside and out,…You know exactly how I was made, bit by bit.*

PSALM 139:15 NASB

The psalmist says that our Master Designer knew all about us from the time we were formed in our mother's womb, and even before we were born. He knew all the days of our individual lives.

We can't begin to number the precious thoughts He has about us—they number more than the grains of sand. You will never find this kind of guarantee on the designer dress labels of the clothes you wear.

—ESTHER BURROUGHS
*Splash the Living Water*

# July 8

*The statutes of the Lord are right, rejoicing the heart; the commandment of the Lord is pure, enlightening the eyes.*

PSALM 19:8

"God has created us and our gifts for a place of His choosing." says Os Guinness, "and we will only be ourselves when we are finally there." Our creative nature is essential to who we are as human beings—as image bearers—and it brings us great joy to live it out with freedom and skill.

Even if it's a simple act such as working on your photo albums or puttering in the garden—these, too, are how we have a taste of what was meant to rule over a small part of God's great kingdom.

*—JOHN ELDREDGE*
*The Journey of Desire*

## June 24

*O Lord, how manifold are Your works! In wisdom You have made them all. The earth is full of Your possessions.*

PSALM 104:24

The only way to describe God's ongoing creative activity is *extravagant*. Thunderclouds gather over the prairies, and afterward He scatters the wildflowers as far as the eye can see. He fills the oceans with orcas and urchins and who knows what. A single maple leaf is woven with greater intricacy than the finest French lace—even though it will fall with the winds of autumn. New stars are born every day; a new sunset painted and swept away each night. Such magnificent generosity.

—JOHN ELDREDGE
*The Journey of Desire*

## July 7

*He who trusts in his riches will fall, but the righteous will flourish like foliage.*

PROVERBS 11:28

We come into life with empty hands—and it is with empty hands that we leave it. Actually we can possess nothing—no property and no person—along the way. It is God who owns everything, and we are but stewards of His property during the brief time we are on earth. Everything that we see about us that we count as our possessions only comprises a loan from God.

— *BILLY GRAHAM*
*Peace with God*

# June 25

*The Lord will give what is good....Righteousness will go before Him, and shall make His footsteps our pathway.*

PSALM 85:12-13

G od—as we all know—does not promise us everything we get it into our minds to hope for. But He does give us reason to believe that what He does promise is a commitment we can rely on. And God's commitment promises much more than possibility.

—LEWIS SMEDES
*Keeping Hope Alive*

# July 6

*Your faithfulness reaches to the clouds. Your righteousness is like the great mountains.*

PSALM 36:5-6

Consider God's faithfulness. His care and concern for His children are stubborn and unyielding. No matter what you do or what happens to you, He will be with you forever. Consider His righteousness. It is immense and infinite, perfect in every way. You can trust Him wholeheartedly for every aspect of life.

—PETER WALLACE
*What the Psalmist Is Saying to You*

# June 26

*I am the God of your father Abraham; do not fear, for I am with you.*

GENESIS 26:24

Hope is not what you expect; it's what you would never dream. It's a wild, improbable tale with a pinch-me-I'm-dreaming ending. It's Abraham adjusting his bifocals so he can see not his grandson, but his son. It's Moses standing in the promised land not with Aaron or Miriam at his side, but with Elijah and the transfigured Christ.

Hope is not a granted wish or a favor performed; no, it's far greater than that. It's a zany, unpredictable dependence on a God who loves to surprise us out of our socks and be there in the flesh to see our reaction.

— MAX LUCADO
*God Came Near*

## July 5

*In the fear of the Lord there is strong confidence, and*
*His children will have a place of refuge.*

PROVERBS 14:26

Chances are good your life has grown more complicated than it was ten years ago, or for that matter, even five years ago. Over time you've collected more and more stuff, taken on more and more debt, accepted more and more responsibilities. Now your spiritual well is dry.

Taking time to discover what really matters is essential…. Don't wait for the doctor to say you've got six months to live. Long before anything that tragic becomes a reality, grow roots deep into the soil of things that really matter.

— *CHARLES R. SWINDOLL*
*Paul: A Man of Grace and Grit*

# June 27

*If you abide in me, and my words abide in you, ask for whatever you wish, and it will be done for you.*

JOHN 15:7

This "abide in me" is the all-inclusive condition for effective intercession. It is the key for prayer in the name of Jesus…. As we live this way, we develop what Thomas à Kempis calls "a familiar friendship with Jesus." We become accustomed to His face. We distinguish the voice of the true shepherd from that of religious hucksters in the same way professional jewelers distinguish a diamond from glass imitations—by acquaintanceship. When we have been around the genuine article long enough, the cheap and the shoddy become obvious.

—RICHARD FOSTER
*Prayer: Finding the Heart's True Home*

*July 4*

*God did not send His Son into the world to condemn the world,*
*but that the world through Him might be saved.*

JOHN 3:17

The word "benevolence" is derived from the combination of the Latin prefix *bene,* which means "well" or "good," and the Latin root that means "will." Together the prefix and the root mean "goodwill."

The Incarnation was an expression of the goodwill of God. His benevolent love. Christ came into the world not only by the will of the Father but by the *goodwill* of the Father.

— R. C. SPROUL
*Loved By God*

# June 28

*I will be merciful to their unrighteousness,*
*and their sins...I will remember no more.*

HEBREWS 8:12

Wow! Now, *that* is a remarkable promise. God doesn't just forgive, He forgets. He erases the board. He destroys the evidence. He burns the microfilm. He clears the computer. He doesn't remember my mistakes. For all the things He does do, this is one thing He refuses to do. He refuses to keep a list of my wrongs.

—MAX LUCADO
*God Came Near*

## July 3

*Work out your own salvation with fear and trembling.*

PHILIPPIANS 2:12

It would have been nice if God had let us order life like we order a meal. I'll take good health and a high IQ. I'll pass on the music skills, but give me a fast metabolism…would've been nice. But it didn't happen. When it came to your life on earth, you weren't given a voice or a vote.

But when it comes to life after death, you were. In my book that seems like a good deal. Wouldn't you agree?

—MAX LUCADO
*He Chose the Nails*

## June 29

*He who trusts in the Lord, mercy shall surround him.*

PSALM 32:10

At times, God requires a season of waiting before He sends His blessing. Then trust becomes your greatest asset. If you don't trust God with your need, you will cry out in fear and panic. At one point during a storm on the Sea of Galilee, the disciples thought they would perish. But Jesus commanded the wind and waves to be still. He taught those men how to trust Him even in the most tempestuous of circumstances, and He is teaching you to watch and wait for His outstretched arm.

— CHARLES STANLEY
*Into His Presence*

## July 2

*No good thing will He withhold from those who walk uprightly.*
PSALM 84:11

Patience is the powerful capacity of selfless love to suffer long under adversity. It is that noble ability to bear with either difficult people or adverse circumstances without breaking down. Over and beyond all of these, patience is that powerful attribute that enables a man or woman to remain steadfast under strain, not just standing still but pressing on.

—PHILLIP KELLER
*A Gardener Looks at the Fruits of the Spirit*

# June 30

*As many of you as were baptized into Christ have put on Christ.*

GALATIANS 3:27

You read it right. We have "put on" Christ. When God looks at us He doesn't see us; He sees Christ. We "wear" Him. We are hidden in Him; we are covered by Him. As the song says "Dressed in His righteousness alone, faultless to stand before the throne."

Presumptuous, you say? Sacrilegious? It would be if it were my idea. But it isn't; it's His.

— MAX LUCADO
*He Chose the Nails*

## July 1

*Every branch that bears fruit He prunes, that it may bear more fruit.*

JOHN 15:2

Submitting to God's pruning can be painful. Yielding requires persistent faith. We must hold tightly to God's character with tears in our eyes. But our Master Gardener is trustworthy. He loves us too much to elevate looking good above being good. With each cut of His "pruning knife." God thins our lives in order to thicken our character.

—ALICIA BRITT CHOLE

*Pure Joy*